MEDITATION

INQUIRY *into the* SELF

James Swartz

SHINING
WORLD

ShiningWorld.com

Fifth edition

Meditation: Inquiry into the Self by James Swartz

Printed in the United States of America 2019

ISBN-13: 978-0-9674444-5-1

ISBN-10: 0-9674444-5-4

Fourth edition

Meditation: Inquiry into the Self by James Swartz

Printed in the United States of America 2018

ISBN-13: 978-1-9820755-7-6

ISBN-10: 1-9820755-7-0

Third edition

Meditation: Inquiry into the Self by James Swartz

Printed in the United States of America 2017

ISBN-13: 978-1-9811184-0-3

ISBN-10: 0-9674444-0-3

Second edition

Meditation: Inquiry into the Self by James B. Swartz

Printed in the United States of America 1999

ISBN-13: 978-0-9674444-0-6

ISBN-10: 0-9674444-0-3

First edition

Meditation: an inquiry into the self by James Bender Swartz

Printed in the United States of America 1999

ISBN-13: 978-0-0000077-0-4

ISBN-10: 0-0000077-0-6

Diagrams by James Swartz

Cover and book design by Robert Grey

Contents

CHAPTER I
Meditation: Inquiry *into the* Self

The Joy Is Not in the Object

THE BUSINESS OF life is the business of happiness. Because we feel limited with respect to happiness, everyone is fully engaged every minute trying to attain happiness. When I take a job, fall in love, read a book, eat a meal, go to the dentist, pray or meditate I expect the activity and/or its results to make me feel better than I do at the moment. No matter how good I feel I can always imagine a state of greater happiness. If I am miserable, my actions will be calculated to remove or lessen the misery, a situation I view as an increase in happiness. When a better state is inconceivable, I refrain from activities that might compromise it. The world's tropical beaches are packed with people flat on their backs, not moving a muscle.

Everything is done for the sake of happiness. Some accumulate money, not necessarily for itself, but for the happiness it supposedly brings. Others seek happiness in life-threatening sports because they produce a high, an aliveness beyond the normal state. We ingest chemicals, pills, drink and drugs to change our state of mind for the better. Belief in God is not intended to make one miserable. Nobody gets married to suffer.

At first glance happiness seems to be the result of activities. I jog, garden, meditate or ski and feel happy. But if happiness were in an activity, the activity should produce happiness for anyone who performed it. Giving away millions makes philanthropists happy. Letting go of a dime is anathema to a miser. A granny who knits for fun will not take pleasure in bungee jumping.

Can happiness be achieved by getting and possessing certain objects? A man divorces his wife because she seems to be the cause of his misery, but before the ink is dry on the divorce decree he finds her in the arms of another – who sees her as his darling bundle of joy. A steak makes a carnivore happy, a vegetarian unhappy. In spite of this sad fact, we slave overtime to get happiness through objects and activities.

Some try to attain happiness through the mind. Poets, writers, artists and intellectuals find happiness playing with thoughts and ideas, feelings and emotions. Professionals, convinced that sustained happiness can be gained through knowledge, subject their minds to years of training and their lives to untold sacrifices.

A tiny minority, spiritual questers, try to find happiness by disciplining themselves with prayer, meditation, chanting, breathing or "processing" to achieve altered or high states of consciousness.

The psychological world believes happiness can be attained by removing subjective barriers – disturbing experiences and memories, self-limiting concepts and unforgiving thoughts lodged in the subconscious mind.

The Limitation of Object Happiness

Both approaches, the physical and the psychological, share the belief that self-effort can alter the objective and subjective factors inhibiting happiness and bring about greater happiness. Conventional wisdom supports this view, and the kernel of truth it contains probably accounts for the universal attempt to get happiness by changing our objective and subjective worlds.

Why do we feel happy when we realize a goal or obtain a desired object? According to spiritual science, all activities are caused by a split from our natural state of happiness, a separation that engenders two apparently contradictory instincts, fear and desire, which cause many disturbing emotions. Beneath every desire a fear lurks, behind every fear a desire. If I don't get what I want I will be unhappy. Avoiding what I do not want makes me happy. So the fear of unhappiness is just the desire for happiness. These two primal forces – which cause attraction and repulsion, attachment and aversion, likes and dislikes – color every aspect of our lives.

The many subtle and gross fears and desires playing in the mind stem from a deeper need, **the need to be free of fear and desire,** the need to be fulfilled or happy. When I say I want a new car or a new lover, I do not actually want the object. I want the happiness apparently wrapped up in it.

Removing the Wall

If happiness or unhappiness does not come from objects, it has to be coming from me.

If this is true, why does it seem to come from objects?

Because the attainment of desired objects or the avoidance of feared objects temporarily removes the wall of fear and desire separating us from the Self, the source of happiness. When the dam breaks, our lives are flooded with happiness, from the ecstasies of love to the pleasure of a cup of coffee.

When a fear or desire is removed, the mind associates the happiness with the object rather than with the removal of the subjective limitation.

That human beings are universally attached to and frightened of physical, emotional and intellectual objects confirms this poorly appreciated truth.

At one time or another almost everyone believes people-love is happiness. As long as the love object gives and receives according to the subject's special needs, everything is fine. But as soon as the object stops cooperating, the love dries up and the removal of the object is then thought to make one happy. Why does the love dry up? Because the idea that it was coming from the object acted like a switch which closed the door between the mind and the Self, effectively cutting off contact with the inner source of love.

That switch, the belief that the joy is in the object, can also pull down the wall. For example, loneliness often causes us to fantasize an ideal someone who is capable of removing our unhappiness. When reality presents an approximation of the fantasy, the wall encompassing the inner ocean breaches, and love cascades wildly into the heart, producing the experience of happiness. Because the process is unconscious and takes place instantaneously, the love seems to be coming from the object or an interaction with the object, but the person is only a catalyst, a trigger activating the inner switch.

Let us argue that since everyone's innermost nature is happiness/love, the joy is in the object, in this case people. True, love is all-pervasive and has to be in the object, but since objects invariably impose conditions on their love, we cannot count on it to make us happy. To avoid this trap I should understand that though love is in everyone, I can only rely on it when I have realized that it is my own Self. To do that **I need to sacrifice the fears and desires separating me from my own happiness/love.** For example, people are happy in deep sleep because objective and subjective limitations do not hamper their experience of bliss.

An Important Definition

What is an object? Spiritual science divides creation into two apparently separate categories: subject and object. Though many subjects seem to exist, there is only one, the Self, and many objects. An object therefore is anything perceived or seen, including the instruments of experience, the senses, mind and intellect. So objects include physical forms, activities, sensations, feelings, thoughts, ideas, beliefs, opinions, memories, dreams and states of mind – like desire and fear. All our life experiences, solicited and unsolicited, are objects. Objects are not conscious, but the Self, the Seer, is. Though egos are subjective with reference to the objects they experience, they are objects from the Self's point of view. The appearance of many individuals is caused by an unconscious association of the one Self with many bodies.

One aim of Self-inquiry is to remove the belief that the joy we seek is in objects.

Object Happiness Is Not Permanent

If you are not convinced that happiness and unhappiness do not reside in objects and activities, you will probably agree that object-related happiness is impermanent. If permanent happiness were attainable by possessing and enjoying objects, the desire to have another object would never arise once the desired object was attained. Conversely if permanent happiness were attainable by the removal of an object (including states of mind like negative feelings), we would never have to rid ourselves of another object. But experience shows that **desire for and fear of objects continue, often increase, with their possession and enjoyment.** I may want more of them, less of them or something else altogether. One day I may even want something I previously believed would make me miserable. The satisfaction of my desires and the removal of my fears does not leave me permanently satisfied. For example, people who associate happiness with a certain object, say a drug- or alcohol-induced state of mind, try to achieve that state over and over, up to and often beyond the point where it no longer yields pleasure. Nobody is ever permanently satisfied by a successful sexual encounter or any other supposedly happiness-producing object or activity. In fact happiness-producing objects and activities often suddenly produce unhappiness.

The confusion about the nature of happiness and unhappiness with reference to objects suggests that the question of **happiness and unhappiness must be centered on me, the subject.**

Am I whole and complete, and therefore immune to the pull of objects or am I an incomplete being, one desperately in need of things to complete me? Having eliminated objects as the source, a confusion still exists about my nature, prompting further analysis. When I think about it, I can see that sometimes I am happy and sometimes unhappy. After careful consideration I can confidently conclude that happiness is natural to me because I always cling to it when I have it. And when I am unhappy the reverse is true: I try feverishly to rid myself of it.

Therefore if I am happy by nature, do not consistently experience happiness and know it does not come from objects and activities, how would I attain it?

I know that through effort I can attain something I do not have, but how would I attain something I do have? When she answered the phone, the secretary put her pencil behind her ear. After a lengthy conversation during which many important subjects were discussed, she began searching for the lost pencil. A co-worker asked why she was agitated, and upon discovering the reason, revealed the pencil's location. In this case the physical search was ineffective, because she had the object all along. And she found it the only possible way – through knowledge. Similarly, if I do not know happiness is my nature, the discovery will only come through knowing, not through doing. Meditation, an inquiry into happiness, is a method of Self-discovery that can lead to knowing.

What Is Happiness?

Let us capitalize Happiness to distinguish it from object happiness. Like its synonym love, Happiness is difficult to define. Often only negatives suffice.

Happiness is the absence of unhappiness, pain, suffering, sorrow. Is it a then kind of neutral, blank state?

No, not at all. One feels very good, but the feeling is not connected with the presence or absence of anyone or anything. Happiness is a causeless, objectless, unspecified sense of well-being. Though not an emotion, it uplifts the emotions.

But are not feelings temporary?

Feelings are fleeting, but the "feeling" of true or real Happiness is not. "True" means it lasts forever. "Real" means unchanging, undying.

Happiness is the sense that nothing is missing or lacking on any level, inwardly or outwardly; that no matter what, one is perfectly equipped to deal with whatever life has to offer.

Happiness is the feeling of endless possibility, invincibility and unqualified freedom seen in children before they've been compromised by conditioning.

Happiness is wholeness, completeness, an unshakable conviction that nothing can be gained or lost. Even if someone or something very dear is taken away, one is undiminished.

Happiness is the knowledge that one is more powerful than all the objects in the world and all the thoughts in one's own mind.

It is the knowledge that no separation exists between oneself and the world, between oneself and others.

Happiness is unconditional, disinterested love for the sake of the beloved.

It is fearlessness, fullness, inexhaustible inner abundance.

And the absence of desire, **especially the absence of desire.**

Happiness, beyond the intellect and unaffected by time, is "the peace that passeth understanding."

Happiness is consciousness, our very essence, not thoughts and feelings, but the awareness[1] illumining thoughts and feelings, the "state of meditation,"[2] the Self, an unshakable identity beyond the body and mind.

We meditate for the same reason we engage in any activity: the belief that it will make us happier than we are. So the only questions remaining are: Does it work? Does it produce temporary happiness or lasting Happiness?

Meditations
1. THE BLANK MIND

An idea that never seems to die says the "state" of meditation, the state of permanent happiness, is a mind free of thoughts. Who gets credit for this theory is a mystery. Perhaps the author analyzed deep sleep and concluded that where thoughts and emotions were absent limitless bliss was present, ergo if thoughtlessness works in deep sleep, why not transpose it to the waking state?

Two facts somehow got lost. If you want to be happy, go to sleep. And limitless bliss is already available in the thought-free "state" of meditation.

The "peak experience" phenomenon lends credence to the Blank Mind theory. During these experiences the mind stops inexplicably and the individual feels wonderfully focused, fearless, peaceful, powerful, aware and loving. Many of the definitions of Happiness in the above list apply to peak experiences. When one feels excellent, one would like to "maintain"[3] the feeling forever. I once encountered a young Japanese man in the *ashram* of an Indian *yogi* who claimed his mind stopped as he skied down Mount Fuji. He said he lived like a king for four years, but when it started up again he was so distraught he quit his job, left his family and set out in search of enlightenment.

In the thirty years I have been involved with meditation I have never met anyone who permanently attained the thought-free state of mind, with the excep-

---

1. Because we have been conditioned to think of Consciousness as mind or thought-flow ("stream of consciousness"), it might be helpful to refer to it as awareness. The mind is pure Consciousness taking the form of perception, thought, feeling, memory, will, etc. – like an ocean taking the form of waves.

2. Because Consciousness is non-dual, it has no "states," but it seems to because of the projections of the mind. See "The Waker, Dreamer and Deep Sleeper" later in this chapter. Thinking of it as a "state" is attractive to those who have a problem with Consciousness as God, a conscious being. However, "states," as we ordinarily understand the term, change and are also not conscious. The Self is unchanging and conscious. It *is* being, but not *a* being.

3. Happiness or meditative states of mind cannot be "maintained," because they are not under anybody's control.

tion of a man who botched his suicide and ended up in a permanent coma. This is because "stopping" the mind is an egoic activity. The results of ego's activities are limited because ego is limited.[4]

Additionally, the mind is just a bundle of thoughts and feelings, and the desire to stop the mind merely another thought in it. How will it eat up the existing thoughts? In fact it will fatten, not starve, the mind.

Finally, how will we work out what needs to be worked out if the mind is not available? True freedom and lasting Happiness are only attained through the knowledge "I am Happiness itself," an impossibility with a non-functioning mind.

Still, a modified Blank Mind theory can produce a reasonably peaceful mind. That certain thoughts and feelings apparently cause suffering is well-documented.[5] For example, desire is the primary link in a chain of inherently frustrating mental phenomena that disturb the mind and generate endless ego-centered activities, which in turn cause *vasanas*[6] that recycle the desire. Refusing to act out ten percent of one's desires over time results in a corresponding reduction of mental, emotional and physical activity, and a ten percent increase of peace. Also, many thoughts and feelings are quite wonderful, do not conflict with happiness and need not be eliminated. So the application of a soft version of the Blank Mind theory can eliminate much suffering.

2. HAPPY THOUGHTS

Most meditation theories are not as radical as the Blank Mind. Not many are willing to go to the trouble of stopping or controlling the mind for limited happiness. Another theory suggests replacing unhappy thoughts with happy thoughts. Affirmations, a popular modern meditation practice, involves making positive statements about oneself or the world. This approach, which is rather like watching a sunset, seems easier than going for a blank mind, but creating and maintaining Happy Thoughts is hard work, so happiness is held hostage to incessant effort. Since personal effort and its results are limited, the happiness produced by this technique would necessarily be limited.

---

4. When the Self is realized, however, it is experienced as thought-free. If the Self is empty and I am the Self, I experience silence, peace, love, power, etc. no matter what the mind is doing.

5. Actually, identification with unhealthy thoughts, not the thoughts themselves, causes suffering.

6. Subconscious impressions. For a detailed discussion of the *vasanas*, see Chapter II.

And when you think about it, creating Happy Thoughts is actually just another way of saying "I am unhappy" and thereby reinforcing the view of oneself as an incomplete being. When you are happy, unhappy thoughts are not a bother. Supposedly the Happy Thoughts crowd out their unhappy companions, but negative thoughts and feelings should not be dismissed out of hand, because they indicate what needs work. In fact because mental and emotional pain is a symptom of a much deeper complaint, the separation from the source of happiness, trying to correct the symptom without addressing the cause is ultimately futile.

However, visualization, a Happy Thought variant, which utilizes the mind's tendency to think in images, can help purify the mind. Since relative happiness is proportional to the degree of mental and emotional purification, any technique that cleanses the mind is useful. Whether such practices lead to lasting Happiness is questionable.

Many New Age visualizations invented by neophytes and created solely from imagination, beyond an immediate feel-good factor are spiritually pointless, because they are not based on a clear understanding of the relationship of the psyche to the Self. Symbolic images need to be powerful Self archetypes, the contemplation of which clears the mind and brings single-pointed attention to the Self.

The meditator who cannot relate to the sophisticated visualizations offered by Eastern religions should at least study their underlying psychology before attempting his or her own. The most common type of visualization involves the contemplation of an enlightened being, a god or goddess.

The purpose of creating a god-like or goddess-like figure in the center of one's consciousness is to symbolize the god-like and/or goddess-like nature of the meditator, the state of pure meditation. A god or goddess is essentially a human being endowed with qualities of compassion, wisdom, discrimination, dispassion, radiance, power and beauty, qualities that are undeveloped in the meditator. "Center" refers to the Self, the center of one's being, and indicates what is most essential. Put a smile on your goddess and you are symbolizing bliss, our innermost nature. Crown her to contemplate the dominion the Self enjoys over your thoughts and feelings. A many-armed god symbolizes the Self's infinite capabilities, its power to accomplish anything. A sword in one hand could indicate discrimination, the ability to separate the real from the unreal. A staff means authority, support. The Self is the ultimate authority and our only true support. Your deity's posture needs to suggest grace and poise, and its gestures to invoke reassuring and kind feelings. A kneeling figure represents devotion,

a reclining one, peace. Colors play an important part in visualization. Gold, for example, symbolizes spiritual wealth; blue, infinity; red, the fire of knowledge or the heat of meditation; green, healing. A natural setting symbolizes the Self as the most natural aspect of oneself. A figure sitting on a high place indicates the exalted, witnessing nature of consciousness. Put your god and goddess in sexual union to symbolize enlightenment, the union of love and wisdom. Or create an androgynous figure to indicate gender transcendence. A god treading on or seated on an animal might symbolize transcendence of the lower nature.

As you meditate on your god or goddess, imagine that its mind is the essence of perfect wisdom. See immaculate rays of light emanating from its heart dispelling unforgiving and self-limiting concepts. Mentally prostrate to your creation, offer loving feelings and ask that it guide you to enlightenment.

3. MANTRA MEDITATION

"Meditation is the uninterrupted thinking of one thought."
~ Patanjali

Mantra is a variation of the Happy Thought style of meditation.[7] A *mantra* is a spiritually charged sound syllable or syllables which, when repeated with feeling and full awareness, can purify the nervous system, eat thoughts and feelings, and awaken the mind to the source of Happiness, the Self.

Mantra meditation is based on the idea that thought is natural to the mind and that the type of thoughts determines our knowledge and experience. According to this theory, the mind becomes what it meditates on. If it constantly thinks of a pleasurable or painful experience, for example, it will become painful or pleasurable. If it meditates on the Self, it will come to know and experience the Self. However, for the mind to accurately think about an object, it must know what and where the object is. Therefore **before it can successfully meditate, it must be turned away from objects and fixed on the Self.**

Mantra first represents the Self with a sound symbol. The mind is then trained to concentrate exclusively on that symbol. When the concentration is perfect, the symbol dissolves into the Self.

The feel-good factor is the upside and the downside of *Mantra* meditation. *Mantras* are composed of "seed" syllables, fine vibrations that activate the bliss

---

7. For more on *mantras*, see "Mantra and Visualization" later in this chapter.

aspect of the Self. Unless there is an inclination to chant endlessly, chanting is a limited solution to the question of lasting Happiness. Yet bliss calms the mind and aids concentration. When concentration is highly developed and directed to the Self, enlightenment is possible.

Mantra as Contemplation

Mantras have specific spiritual meanings, the consistent and deep contemplation[8] of which can lead to liberation. Chanted daily by tens of millions worldwide, *Om namah Shivaya* is a popular *mantra*. What does it mean? The first word, *Om*,[9] is the Vedic sound symbol of the Self, pure consciousness. The knowledge in the "What Is the Self?" section above applies to *Om*. *Om* is generic consciousness, not an attribute or quality. It is customarily chanted at the beginning and end of every meditation because it exists before the beginning and after the end of everything.

The second word, one found in many *mantras*, is *namah*. If *Om* refers to universal consciousness, *namah* refers to the individual. It's not a name of the individual, but a statement of the relationship between the individual and the Self. *Namah* is composed of two syllables, *na* and *ma*. *Na* means "not." *Ma* means "me." So *namah* means "not me" and informs me that I am not exclusively the limited self. Contemplation of *namah* negates the limited self. The negation of the limited self is called surrender. I am prostrating to my universal Self, acknowledging it as my sole support, as the real "me."

The Effect Is the Cause

Thinking of oneself as an unlimited being is not delusional. Certainly the body and mind are limited, but the essential consciousness, that without which we do not exist, is non-separate from the consciousness in everyone and everything. How far is the wave from the ocean?

If *Om* and *namah* bubble with meaning, *Shivaya*[10] overflows. Both *Shivaya* and *Om* symbolize the Self. But *Shivaya* adds another dimension to our contemplation of *Om*. It means "that which is always auspicious." What is it about us that is always good? The fact that we exist. Throw away everything, even the body, but who will throw you away? That which is always good, you, is reality.

---

8. Contemplation of the inner meaning, not the mere verbal repetition, gives the *mantra* its power.

9. The meaning of *Om* is the subject of the twelve *mantras* of the *Mandukya Upanishad*.

Good doesn't mean the opposite of bad, but indicates the Self's substantial and limitless nature.

4. INSIGHT MEDITATION

Insight meditation[11] requires neither a blank mind, generating special imagery nor repeating a *mantra*, but trains the mind to dispassionately observe the phenomena constantly appearing on its luminous screen. This ancient and respectable meditation trains the meditator not to identify with, react to or act out *samskara*-motivated[12] impulses. The realization of the impermanence of all phenomena and the discovery of the non-existence of ego that comes from dispassionate observation causes knotty problems to unravel, freeing the mind of limitations. An unlimited mind is a happy mind.

The theory is sound, but will the mind remain free as a result of such a practice? Only when the unconscious,[13] the source of experience, is emptied. Because the quantity of stuff in the unconscious is unknown, fulfillment may be postponed indefinitely. Secondly, although problems are solved, what is to insure that one will not generate new *samskaras*, and therefore new problems? The unconscious is not merely a passive memory like intellect, but it is a dynamic mechanism that recycles everything created by the ego/mind entity. Only by neutralizing the *vasanas*, the seeds sprouting from past actions, a Herculean task, can the mind be freed.[14] Furthermore, to "maintain" the round-the-clock awareness that might make the technique work in the long run is virtually impossible.

Finally, if witnessing is the result of splitting the mind, training one part to observe the other, the split will need to be healed, so witnessing meditations eventually have to deal with the removal of the witness. If witnessing is maintained by effort, the benefits will cease when the witnessing stops, the witness

10. Pronounced "she-vai-yuh."

11. Known as *vipassana*, a technique dating back to the time of the Buddha and earlier.

12. Subconscious formations, related to *vasanas*. See Chapter II.

13. See Chapter II.

14. The method for insuring against creating new subconscious impressions is explained in the "*Karma Yoga*" section of Chapter III.

being a self-appointed voyeur who, for reasons of its own, keeps a hard eye trained on the mind's seductions.

Still, *vipassana*, which mimics the power of consciousness, is based on a scientific fact: when you watch something for an extended period, awareness turns around and becomes aware of itself, the Witness.[15] Practiced with an inquiry into the nature of the Witness, it can awaken one to the knowledge "I am effortless awareness. I am Happiness itself." Short of that, *vipassana* is an excellent, though arduous, technique for purifying painful *samskaras*[16] and attaining a relatively peaceful state of mind.

5. THE GAP

Another theory defines meditation as attention to the space between thoughts, or the Gap, between the waking and sleep states. That, contrary to appearances, nothing in the universe is substantial is the basis of this technique. A material object, though seemingly solid to the senses, strings out into waves and completely loses form upon closer analysis. Similarly, the mind, which is capable of thinking only one thought at a time, is an apparently opaque flow of thought. Yet gaps exist between each thought – a moment after a thought ends, its successor begins. Since the omnipresent and all-pervasive Self is the substrate on which the mind dances, it pervades the space between thoughts. Therefore if the unconscious *karmic* pressure that jams up the thoughts were reduced, the thoughts would slow down and bring about a heightened state of awareness, allowing the meditator to see into the Gap and realize the Self.

The idea combines nicely with *mantra*, a conscious thought. Most mental activity is unconscious patterns of quasi-logical associations specific to the *samskara* sprouting in the mind at any time. Associative thinking, where one thought connects to another like a link in a chain, is spiritually useless, because the mind can end up anywhere. But *mantra* is a specific conscious thought about the Self introduced into the mind in place of everyday thoughts and practiced with a Gap. If the *mantra* is not simply interjected between random thoughts or chanted on top of the *samskara*-produced associations, but allowed to absorb the mind's energy and become the only thought, stopping it stops the mind momentarily and, at that moment, if attention is directed to the Gap, the Self in the form of silence, peace, light or energy is experienceable.

15. The Self.

16. The purification techniques are discussed in Chapter III.

Meditation on the interval between waking and sleep, when the waking ego is dissolving into its constituent elements, is another Gap meditation. If awareness can be maintained when the mind/ego entity dies, as it does immediately prior to sleep, one can "enter" the Self through this gateway.

6. PAY ATTENTION!

A final theory, one that makes a good deal of sense, is meditation as attention. Attention is not a specific thought but the flow of awareness to a particular object, like the flow of oil through a wick to the flame. In this type of meditation, of which an example will be given later, the attention is moved from the sense world to the breath and finally fixed on the Self.

Who Am I?

Whether it comes through a meditation technique or another avenue, **the rediscovery[17] of oneself as effortless awareness beyond the mind, rather than a watching ego or the watched mind, is enlightenment, the goal of meditation practice.**[18] "Beyond" doesn't mean somewhere else, but the awareness by which the ego/mind is known.

The relationship between the Self and the mind is sometimes likened to the relationship between the sun and the moon. The moon-like mind is a seemingly sentient bundle of inert tendencies, thoughts and feelings because it is illumined by the sun-like Self, the radiant Spirit.[19]

---

17. Because the Self is the most essential part of our experience, it is known. However, owing to the pressure of the *samskaras*, the mind extroverts and forgets the Self, so when one "realizes the Self" or "attains enlightenment," it is never a new experience but a "recognition," a "rediscovery" or a "reawakening."

18. Enlightenment and Self-realization are synonyms. However, in spiritual literature the constant experience of the Self by a purified mind is called either Self-realization or enlightenment. A slightly subtler and final stage in which the meditating mind "merges" into the Self is also termed either enlightenment or Self-realization. In the first stage, the Self is the object of meditation, and in the second, the mind is the object because the meditator has "merged" into the Self. In reality there is no merger, because the meditator is already the Self. Stage II follows effortlessly from Stage I as long as the mind holds steady on the Self. The transition is effortless because the mind understands that the Self is the source of limitless happiness and clings to it with a vengeance.

19. Capitalized words are roughly synonymous and refer to the Self.

I Am the Light of the World

Though the Self cannot be accurately described, it can be known because it is us. Always present and accounted for, consciousness is the most familiar and essential part of every experience. However, because it cannot be objectified, we do not know it the way we know ideas, emotions or sense objects, aspects of outer reality known through media. If we are looking for the lasting Happiness that comes with liberation, even knowledge of scripture will not do the trick, because it would only be inferential, conditioned by how an admittedly ignorant intellect interpreted certain ideas. If Self-knowledge is not mediate intellectual knowledge, what kind is it?

Experience versus Knowledge

Knowledge takes place in the intellect, but not all knowledge is "intellectual." Intellectual knowledge is knowing of something about which one has no experience. Knowledge not backed up by experience is not knowledge, it is opinion or belief. However, concluding that because knowledge can be intellectual it is spiritually useless is foolish because the intellect definitely needs knowledge to make an inquiry into the Self.

For knowledge to happen, the mind needs to contact an object of knowledge. Contact with the object is experience. But the knowledge half of the experience only happens if the intellect is alert and paying attention to the experience. For example, if the ego is completely wrapped up in the feelings and sensations arising during an experience, the intellect will not work properly and knowledge will not happen. For this reason accident victims cannot accurately report what happened, for example. A similar phenomenon occurs in commonplace situations when intense concentration on something prevents knowledge of events taking place in the immediate environment.

It stands to reason therefore that if the Self is the object of experience, and I am so "blissed out" or excited when the experience is taking place that my intellect is turned off, I will be unable to know the Self.

Because the intellect was unavailable during Self-experience, many are left with vague and often confusing feelings of wonder, and are not freed of the craving for experience that is the signature of enlightenment. When you realize that you are the bliss you are experiencing, experience continues but **the longing for blissful experience dries up.**

Often a mystic experience of the Self in the form of a vision of God or a particular deity leaves the impression that the Self is the deity or that the deity caused the experience. However, since experience of the deity is fleeting, when the deity is not manifesting, a craving for its return dominates the mind, even though Self-experience is actually going on all the time "at a deeper level."

Whether the Self can be an object of experience is the subject of a long-standing spiritual controversy. Some claim it cannot be experienced, others that it can. If Self-realization is described as an experience, a transaction between subject and object, it is a peculiar experience. Ordinary experience is a straight-forward interaction between a human being and its world. If the mind,[20] consciousness with a small "c," is a gross and limited transformation of pure Consciousness, how will it fully know or experience pure Consciousness, the Self, in its subtle, unlimited form? Just as the senses cannot experience the mind, nor the material world the senses, the mind/ego entity cannot "experience" the Self.

According to spiritual science even the material world is a transformation of Consciousness. But as Consciousness involves itself with itself as matter, its "light," or awareness, seemingly gets absorbed into the objects and, on the physical level at least, apparently stops shining. For example, even though light reflecting off my body falls equally on a mirror and the black wall on which the mirror hangs, I will only see myself in the mirror. The Self is also seemingly absorbed into a mind clouded with emotion and thought, making it unexperienceable for all intents and purposes. It can, however, be "experienced" in a mirror-like, pure mind.

The non-experience school claims that humans are two-tiered, existing on one level as a subject interacting with objects, which necessarily means experience, and on another as Consciousness, the "light"[21] illumining experience. So in scriptural literature you will find definitions of the Self as transcendent, beyond, uninvolved and unattached to anything. It will be described as living in its own hermetically-sealed world, the shining world of knowledge, unaware of anything other than itself or alternatively as the witness of outer events.

Many who are unaware of this fact incorrectly believe the ego will experience the Self like it experiences everything else. So to save them the grief of trying to obtain a mind-blowing cosmic enlightenment experience, the knowledge people point out that the Self is not that type of experience. Mind-blowing blissful cosmic experiences, which come by the grace of God, sometimes in

20. The mind is technically called the "subtle body" and is known as the "instrument of experience." "Person, individual, soul" and "human being" are commonly used terms signifying the subtle body. The subtle body is explained in Chapter II.

21. Hence the term "enlightenment," which probably originally meant a mind aware of the light illumining it.

conjunction with conscious spiritual practice, sometimes quite unsolicited, are simply mind-blowing blissful cosmic experiences, reportable only because they are observed by the Self, which just as disinterestedly watches non-mind-blowing, unhappy, mundane experiences.

Thinking of enlightenment as an experience also opens the meditator up to the problem of maintenance. When the ego enjoys a pleasant experience like the Self, it always feels that the experience should continue indefinitely. Apart from the fact that the Self is out of time, and therefore not subject to disappearance, no ego experience lasts forever. If I am unaware of this I am tempted to see if I cannot "maintain" the Self-experience. On the other hand, knowledge requires no maintenance. For example, the knowledge of one's name does not interfere but politely remains in the background as one goes about one's business, effortlessly popping into consciousness on demand. Moreover, Self-experience cannot be made constant, because the Self has no handles. How can the ego, which is a limited form of the Self, hold onto the unlimited Self and make it deliver a particular experience? Additionally, Self-experience cannot be maintained, because it is always present and self-evident. The one who mistakenly wants to maintain the experience is already the Self.

The experience of egolessness is a common definition of enlightenment. Aside from the obvious fact that experience needs an experiencer, an ego – except for the experience of egolessness – what happens when the sense of separateness returns? Is the Self no longer available for experience? It is because it is the only possible experiencer, witnessing both the prior experience of egolessness and the present experience of ego. If it weren't witnessing, how would egolessness be known? Therefore enlightenment does not require any particular experience. It only requires that I remove the notion that I'm not already the Self.

Knowledge has it that the Self is everything. Therefore it is the experiencer, the experienced and the experiencing. It is never apart from us. If this is so, thinking in terms of experience is spiritually unwise, because it may actually prevent one from finding out who one is. For example, if someone experiences the Self for a period of time and the experience stops, the person might be heard to say, "I was the Self for two days." Fair enough, but from this point on the experience becomes an acute source of misery because the Self is no longer available for experience.

Where did the Self go? It did not go anywhere, because it is always present. What went (or never happened) was the knowledge "I am the Self." This knowledge needs to happen if the experience of the Self is to set you free. In other words, I am not the victim of a lack of Self-experience but of the dualistic belief that "I" experience something other than my Self.

If the idea of pure knowledge is too stark and unforgiving, perhaps it will help to think of Self-realization as a knowing experience. Knowing is as much an experience as any physical or psychological transaction with an object. To distinguish it from knowledge of an unexperienced object or knowledge by perception and inference, enlightenment is called "realization," which means "to make practical or real." Making the Self real simply means allowing the knowledge that one is a partless whole to destroy one's sense of limitation.

Self-knowledge will definitely make sense of the whole of one's life, since the Self is the only factor present throughout all one's diverse experiences. Additionally, the idea that an ignorant, experience-hungry ego can properly appreciate the overall meaning of his or her life on the basis of the knowledge gained from disparate experiences is ridiculous. A gem dealer visited a flea market where he found a huge uncut opal on the table of a man who had picked it up on a camping trip, thinking it was just an interesting rock. For ten dollars the vendor relinquished the opal, which subsequently sold for two million dollars. Both vendor and customer experienced the rock, but only one knew its true value – **because knowledge was operating in his mind.**

Where is this knowledge going to come from if I don't have it already? I do have it already, but not in the form of opinions and beliefs about the meaning of my experiences. It resides secretly in the Self and is made available to me in at least two interrelated ways: through the teaching tradition and through meditation, direct contact of **a tutored and purified mind** with the Self. The techniques for gaining this kind of mind are revealed in Chapter III. Vedanta, the teaching tradition, uses a very clever method of thinking in a formal meditative setting to remove the notion that one is merely a limited, experience-conditioned creature. If the knowledge enshrined in this text were properly understood and used as the basis of a discrimination between the Self and the not-Self in the seat of meditation, enlightenment may happen.

That experience does not always lead to true knowledge is another dimension in the "experience versus knowledge" debate. For example, from the point of view of someone standing on the equator, the sun seems to rise in the east and set in the west, but at certain times of the year the same person can stand on the North Pole and experience the sun going around in a circle. Which is true? Knowledge has it that, although apparently rising and setting with reference to the earth, the sun is actually stationary and it is the earth that turns. Similarly, if the Self is experienced at one time as a blazing light without circumference, for example, and as a cosmic vibration at another, which is true? Knowledge has it that the Self is the awareness illumining both experiences.

Another example of the contradictory nature of experience, psychic fact, is that sometimes we experience ourselves as miserable suffering creatures and sometimes as radiantly happy beings. Which is true? Spiritual science claims that we are miserable, suffering creatures when we are identified with the egoic part of ourselves, and happy, adequate beings when we are identified with the Self, an identification that is not possible without knowledge.

Yet we cannot discount experience, because discrete identifiable Self-experiences are helpful, even though Self-experience is taking place all the time whether we know it or not. Therefore meditation and other spiritual practices are to be encouraged. Additionally, if the knowledge of the Self did not change one's experience, what would be the point of seeking it? The way the enlightened experience[22] the world is radically different from those identified with *samskara*-projected experience. Or more accurately, the Self-realized enjoy a completely different relationship to *samskara*-projected experience than those who don't know the Self.

The Self is an object of desire because it eliminates limitation and inadequacy. Moreover, it is the "sense" of inadequacy buried deep within the mind that knowledge aims to destroy. When the idea that one is inadequate is removed, one's experience changes because what one was previously suffering was nothing more than the idea of inadequacy. Experiencing the Self without the destruction of the idea that one is limited is only marginally superior to other experiences. The so-called spiritual world is little more than millions whose knowledge of themselves as limited beings has survived repeated experiences of the Self.

The purpose of this discussion is not to weigh in on one side or the other of a weighty argument, but to show that we need to appreciate the inadequacy of beliefs and opinions born solely of personal experience. And also, because **so-called "intellectual" knowledge about the Self, its bodies and states, and the methods of purification, is definitely necessary for success in spiritual life.** Without it, the meditator will fail to reap the sweet fruit.

---

22. The enlightened experience the world, their bodies and their minds just like the unenlightened. However, enlightenment grants *viveka*, the power to separate the meaning the mind projects on experience from reality, the Self. Therefore something that seems real to the unenlightened may be known to be unreal by the enlightened.

Finally, meditation technique will not give Self-knowledge, because techniques only produce certain types of experience. Yet a meditation practice that creates the kind of mind that is clear enough to make a disciplined inquiry into the Self and its vehicles is absolutely essential for enlightenment.

The Waker, Dreamer and Deep Sleeper

What if I am denied Happiness because I think I am somebody I am not? The following discussion reveals the reason the "I" I think I am will only experience periodic fits of happiness, never lasting fulfillment.

As humans we have three "egos," or experiencing entities.[23] The waking state ego[24] is Consciousness,[25] the limitless Self, shining through the body-mind-intellect bundle experiencing both the material world and the subtle world of feelings, emotions, thoughts, beliefs, perceptions, ideas, memories, etc.

Everyone primarily views himself or herself as a waker. When I say "me" in conversation, I am referring to myself as a waking state entity. Our analysis will show that the idea of oneself as a waking state entity is a belief accompanied by the erroneous conviction that the waking state and its objects are reality.

The waker's consciousness is turned outward. It is the Self shining through the senses, mind, intellect – illumining objects, emotions and thoughts. Idealistic metaphysics' claim that no world exists apart from the perceiver means that the Self does not see a world unless it shines through a body, mind or intellect, not that the physical world does not exist. Though it exists independently of the waker's perceptions, the universe doesn't exist apart from the Self.

The waker, *vishwa*, is a consumer of experience. Sanskrit literature describes the waker as "the one with thirteen mouths." The "thirteen mouths" refer to the ten senses, mind, intellect and ego. These instruments are mouths in that, powered by the momentum of past experiences, the *samskaras*, they aggressively seek experience. The physical body consumes matter, the four elements[26] in various permutations and combinations. The mind constantly chews

23. The teaching that follows is taken from the *Mandukya Upanishad*, a Vedic text from the pre-Christian era.

24. See the diagram on the next page.

25. The word "Consciousness" as defined in Vedic texts is unmodified consciousness, i.e. the Self without qualities.

26. Air, fire, water and earth.

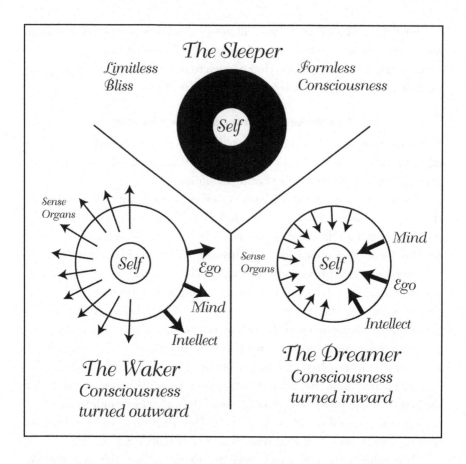

emotion, the intellect eats ideas, and the ego gobbles any experience it believes will make it feel adequate and happy.

Consciousness turned inward[27] is called the dreamer.[28] It enjoys experience similar to the waking state in some respects and radically different in others. In the dream state the Self illumines only subtle objects, a replay of the *vasanas*[29] gathered in the waking state expressing as mental imagery. In the waking state the *vasanas*[30] express as the waker's thoughts and feelings. Like the waker, the

27. In fact Consciousness is all-pervasive and can't turn inward or outward. The consciousness referred to is Consciousness functioning as the mind.

28. The lower right third of the diagram.

29. Subconscious impressions.

dreamer takes itself and its world as reality. The dreamer is equipped with the same instruments of experience as the waker: dream senses to consume dream objects, a dream mind to emote and feel, a dream intellect to think dream thoughts, and a dream ego to go about experiencing the dream life.[31] The *Upanishad* refers to the dreamer as *taijasa,* the "shining one," indicating its nature as Consciousness. Even though the waking senses are inactive, all dreams are bathed in light because the Self, Consciousness, is shining through the dreamer, illumining the dream world, just as it shines through the waker and illumines waking objects.

Sleep is defined as a state, saturated with happiness, where one loses consciousness, does not desire external objects, does not see internal objects and is both Self and self-ignorant.

The sleeper is called *prajna,* or formless consciousness. The sleeper is extremely subtle, virtually unknowable, its existence inferred by the knowledge upon waking that one slept well. People with serious problems like depression often sleep to avoid the limitations that plague them in the waking state. Though the bliss of the Self shines in all states, in the waking and dream states it is broken by sense perceptions and many divisions of thought and feeling. When experience alternates in this way we unconsciously develop a confusing idea of who we are.

The deep sleep, or "seed," state is free of both the waking and dream egos and objects because the *vasanas* projecting them are dormant. When the "seeds" sprout, one becomes a waker or a dreamer, and experiences the appropriate world.

Because we do not remember being conscious in it, the sleep state is often thought to be a void. In fact Sanskrit literature refers to it as "the womb" because our waking and dream worlds emerge from it. When you wake up in the morning your whole life is consistent with the day before, indicating that previous experience had simply entered a dormant state. The dormant potential of the sleep state containing the macrocosmic *vasanas*[32] is called *Isvara,* the

---

30. Chapter II presents a detailed discussion of the *vasanas.*

31. The substance of the dream field, thought and feeling, are drawn from both the macrocosmic and microcosmic minds, i.e. collective and individual experience.

32. The impressions of the experience of all beings over limitless time. Creation, according to Vedanta, is the recycling of unmanifest experience.

Creator, in Vedantic literature. With reference to the microcosmic *vasanas*[33] the sleeper is called *prajna*.

The sleep state is also known as the gateway between the waking and the dream states because it functions as a kind of closet with two doors, where the dreamer can don the guise of the waker in preparation for its appearance on the waking stage and vice versa.

Though they seem to be so, the three selves are not separate entities, but are apparently distinct entities created when the limitless I associates with a given state of consciousness. Associated with the waking state, the Self seemingly becomes a waking state personality, suffering or enjoying the limitations of the senses, mind, intellect, ego, the unconscious and ignorance. The dreamer suffers the limitations of the mind, the unconscious and ignorance. And the sleeper, the Self apparently merged into the unconscious, suffers only ignorance and limitless bliss.

These three states and egos are known to everyone and constitute the totality of the limited I's experience. An interesting question posed by this analysis is: Who am I? If I am the waking ego, the person on my driver's license, what happens to me when I become a sleeper? I willingly surrender my body, mind, intellect and all my physical possessions to become a mass of limitless Consciousness.

Yet I do not seem to be content as a sleeper, the blissfully ignorant subtle being, because I sacrifice that status to suffer and enjoy the world created by my *vasanas* in waking or dream states. My dreamer identity is equally insufficient, because I always leave it to become a waker or a sleeper. So my status as any one ego is uncertain and my true identity open to question.

If identity is happiness, then an ego identity will deliver only intermittent happiness, since the happiness experienced in sleep disappears in the waking state. Dream happiness dissolves on waking, and waking happiness cannot be transported into sleep or dream. For example, one can be quite happy at bedtime, fall asleep and suffer a nightmare or leave the misery of the waking state to enjoy a happy dream.

If I Am Real, I Have to Exist All the Time

The answer to "who am I?" is that I am not any of these egos or ego states. **If I am real, I have to exist all the time.** I cannot suddenly be someone one minute and somebody else the next. I experience life as a single conscious being.

33. The personal subconscious, the impressions of each individual.

In fact I exist in the waking, dream and deep sleep states independently of the waker, dreamer and deep sleeper.

As what?

As the Self, the awareness of and witness to the three states. Aside from meditation, the Self is perhaps easiest to identify in the dream state because the physical senses are inactive and no thoughts arise because of their contact with objects. A dream plays on the screen of the mind like a movie. Though physical light is absent, the dream ego and dream events are clearly illumined, a phenomenon sometimes referred to as "lucid" dreaming. The lucidity is the Self functioning as the dreamer, "the shining one." However, identification with the dream ego and its doings prevents us from properly appreciating the dream light, the Self.

In the waking state too we are so preoccupied with the happenings in our worlds and minds that we are unaware that both the sense objects and our thoughts and feelings are bathed in awareness, the source of happiness.

In deep sleep the ego dissolves into very fine unconscious thought, so it is denied knowledge of the Self even though it enjoys limitless bliss.

Meditation Practice

Meditation practice is the waking state tool connecting us with the Self, unalloyed Happiness, not the goal. Some traditions teach that practice is both and insist that sitting should be enjoyed for itself, quite apart from striving to attain a high state – good advice because transcendence is reluctant to come when called. In fact just sitting still, thinking of nothing in particular, waiting for a bus or driving home after work, might cause transcendence – the experience that the body and mind are merely objects, like the passing scene.

Contrary to popular opinion, transcendence does not have to be experienced as an earth-shattering "out of body" experience. In fact though no one seems to notice, we are already always beyond our bodies and minds. Meditation practice should strip us of the identification with the body and mind, allowing us to appreciate the natural separation of the Self from its vehicles.

Aside from the goal, meditation is practiced for psychological and physical benefits: increased energy, heightened senses and reactions, strengthened immunity, improved intelligence, creativity, efficiency, power, pleasure, discrimination, dispassion, sense of purpose, peace of mind, expanded awareness, selflessness, compassion and others.

What to Expect

Without a powerful technique to quickly lift the mind to the level of the Self, meditation practice is difficult for two reasons. First, until the idea that it should be entertaining is abandoned, practice is deadly boring. The realization that some part wants to sabotage the meditation is a large marquee advertising the whereabouts of an ego whose craving for excitement can quickly derail practice. The ego likes action and entertainment, and will only grudgingly cooperate, since meditation moves it from the center to the periphery of one's consciousness.

Second, observation makes the ego feel exposed and vulnerable. Born in the darkness, unappreciative of scrutiny, it will certainly crank out an incessant stream of distracting thoughts and feelings throughout the meditation. Because of its mindless belief in the virtue of self-validating work, no matter how ill-conceived or illogical, it needs to be given something to do, which accounts for the popularity of active over witnessing meditations.

Active meditations keep the ego busy thinking holy thoughts, saying calming words or visualizing "spiritual" images. Because it bores quickly, its least preferred activity is watching the breath or mind. Sooner rather than later the meditator who listens to the ego will consistently find him or herself mentally sitting on the beach sipping a Coke, reading an adventure novel and working on a tan.

Allowing the ego to preside over meditation practice puts the fox in charge of the chicken coop. Understandably, most initial "spiritual" activity is ego-based, but changes should evolve out of discrimination and dispassion arising from meditative insight and awareness, not as a reaction to suffering or ego "shoulds and shouldn'ts, dos and don'ts." The monasteries, *zendos* and *ashrams* of the world are populated with egos whose fundamental sense of identity has been unaffected by the move to the religious life, unsurprising since ego transcendence is not unlike a salmon swimming hundreds of miles upstream to spawn.

In the next chapter we consider why meditation as a practice is so difficult to master, what causes the incessant cascading of thought and feeling, why deep-seated complexes yield so grudgingly to awareness and why trying to control the mind with the ego is impossible.

A Simple Technique

Based on the idea that the mind likes pleasure and the Self is the ultimate pleasure, the following simple technique introduces the mind to the Self.

If holding the body upright is difficult, lying down is acceptable as long as the tendency to sleep can be overcome when the mind empties. Some go for the full-lotus position, while the less physical gravitate to the half-lotus or the simple meditative poses evolved by *hatha yoga*. In India, where *yoga* evolved, people have no furniture, so sitting cross-legged on the ground is second nature. But if you are forever having to smile benignly through the pain in your lower body because your feet are resting on top of the thighs, it is best to opt for an easy chair. Except for the attempt to awaken dormant energies in the body, a practice not recommended for neophytes, the position of the body is not critical. It should be comfortable, and the meditator should be prepared to take a short vacation.

On the mental level assume a gracious, upright, noble pose. Get into a sensitive, inquiring state of mind, like a botanist patiently examining a delicate flower. The meditator should think of meditation as an afternoon on the beach, not a shift in the mines.

With the eyes closed, settle in.

What is next?

Ask for help. Obviously, if you knew who you were, you would not be meditating in the first place, so by sitting you are really saying you do not know anything, the most essential ingredient for a successful meditation. Most meditators believe in a higher power, God, a spirit guide, *guru* figure, the saints, the universe, "guidance" or a deity. The Self, which knows every thought and feeling, understands the need and will respond through the chosen symbol. The Self put the meditation idea into the mind in the first place, so the meditator needn't worry. Everything that needs to happen will happen.

Make a resolution to leave your worries and involvements behind. It is good to meditate in a place not used for other activities. Feel satisfied that you are making an effort to meditate. Next, clear the mind of memories of previous meditations, good or bad. Trying to improve a bad meditation or reproduce a good one is futile and will agitate the mind.

After the invocation, scan and relax the body from the feet up. If you have a hard time relaxing, use a little visualization. Imagine you are a warm, peaceful, light-filled ball of consciousness inside your feet, and expand until the feet feel hollow. Next, bore your way up the legs, hollowing out the ankles, knees and hips. Take your time. It may seem a silly trick, but it works because the body is actually a vast field of consciousness, not a constipated little ball of meat. If the "ball" does not work, use any method you wish to relax your way up the legs. Because they are associated with waste removal, the stomach and abdominal organs often carry negative energy, so spend sufficient time working in this area. Move up and explore the chest. Its association with the emotional center causes angry and unforgiving feelings to lodge there, so the muscles are often tight. Scan leisurely, leaving it light-filled and relaxed, then move up to the neck and shoulders. Much tension accumulates here, so take your time. When it's relaxed, move out to the tips of the fingers, and hollow out the arms like you did the legs. Then redo the neck and shoulders.

The face we carry around in the world is not usually our real face, so we need to do something to get it back to normal. Work around the chin, mouth and cheeks first, and then up to the eyes and forehead. You will find many tiny vibrations hovering around these regions, so release the muscles supporting them and let them dissipate. A smile or frown means too much energy has been left behind. Aim for the indifferent look of a Buddha or the peaceful face of the dead.

The idea behind all this scanning and relaxing is to prepare the body for your exit. Think of the body as an automobile and yourself as the driver. The driver just returned from a long day on the road, will park the car in the garage and enter his or her home for the evening. Before you park it for good, rescan the whole thing to make sure it is comfortable and turn your attention to the breath.

The Breath

The breath goes in and out nicely on its own. Simply observe it; do not breathe consciously, although observing the breath consciousizes it a bit. Not to worry, it will settle down and return to its normal pattern. The point of meditation is to relax, not just physically but mentally. Watching the breath occupies the mind with a simple rhythmic object. Because it wants glamour and excitement, the mind quickly grows bored, but boring is good. Learning to enjoy boredom is one of the benefits of meditation.

At this point I give the mind a challenge by training my attention to ride on the breath. When the breath is out the attention should flow out, and when the breath comes flowing in the attention comes with it.

Of course the mind will wander. Pull it back and synchronize it with the breath. It need not ride perfectly on every breath. Do not get upset if it doesn't work immediately. Take your time.

Meditation is not about the breath anyway. The breath is only a tool. How long should one work with it? There is no hard and fast rule; sometimes five or ten minutes, sometimes longer. You are looking for a sign that the mind is getting quiet because it stills quickly as it synchronizes with the breath.

As the mind and breath harmonize, use surplus attention to release pent-up thoughts and feelings on the out-breath. Do not relate to or analyze the thoughts/feelings at this point, simply pay attention to what you are doing. Just as the out-breath cleanses the body, releasing thoughts detoxifies the mind. From a meditative perspective, one's relationship to the thoughts is more important than the thoughts themselves. Later, when you are seeing from the Self, you may wish to analyze them, although ultimately all thoughts are basically useless. Do not be concerned about losing them, they will be back. The aim is to take a little pressure off the mind, not empty it completely.

The Silence[34]

The mind is becoming quiet when you become conscious of all sorts of sounds of which you were previously unaware – like going to sleep. You never hear the clock ticking until you want to sleep, because the mind, formerly occupied with its thoughts, is emptying. You may hear the heart beat, the scratching of the breath as it goes in and out, snippets of conversation taking place blocks away, the hum of the kitchen refrigerator, a fly buzzing lazily in an adjoining room. The thoughts may be amplified, larger than life, or slower, as if they were slogging through molasses. You might start picking up on them as they start rather than midway through their cycle.

You will notice these things because you are now surrounded by a bubble of Silence which, depending on the quietude of the mind, is hardly noticeable or roars as it does on the great plains in the dead of a summer night.

When the Silence appears as a tangible presence, take your attention from the breath and fix it on the Silence. Because it has served its purpose, the breath should drop out of consciousness or seem very faint, far away and irrelevant. Occasionally the Silence completely swallows the mind, and you find yourself deep within your Self, unaware of the breath, the noises in the room, your thoughts – absolutely everything – a state similar to conscious sleep. Time dissolves, and you might be overcome with ecstasy.

Many unusual experiences can happen when the mind is quiet. Let them happen, do not cling. All experience, like thought, is essentially transitory, not subject to ego control. Moreover, **the purpose of meditation is not to produce**

---

34. The Silence is not merely the absence of sound or thought. It is the awareness of the absence of sound and thought.

specific pleasurable experiences but to inquire into the nature of the Self and distinguish it from the mind.

When the mind remains partially active and the senses report information, the thoughts and sounds appear into and disappear out of the Silence like phantoms. The silent, peaceful awareness in which they appear is a rock-like, real, luminous and eternal presence. The experience of the Silence is the essence of meditation. It allows the meditator to carefully observe the transitory and insubstantial nature of the body-mind instrument.

I think of the Silence as the altar of the inner temple and take great pleasure in witnessing the thoughts and feelings arise out of and disappear back into it. The discipline of meditation is always the struggle with the ego to keep attention fixed on the Silence. If the Silence is particularly deep or radiant, the ego will be so stunned it will surrender easily like an awestruck child at a carnival. But more often than not its powerful *samskaras* carry attention far afield. **Holding to the Silence for the purpose of inquiring into the nature of the Self is meditation.**

One would not think to visualize or chant, because the experience of the Silence is fascinating and fulfilling. However, sometimes the *mantra* arises spontaneously, chanting itself. Occasionally meditation activates particularly subtle parts of the unconscious, and wonderful visions appear.

The meditation is not creating the Silence, although it may seem so. The Silence is the substrate of experience, self-luminous Consciousness. The technique simply withdraws enough consciousness from the body and mind to allow the ever-present and apparently hidden Silence to manifest.

Once you are consistently able to contact the Silence, start the inquiry. Who or what is the Silence? Who is the meditator? Explore the boundary between the mind and the Silence. The Silence is the most subtle form of the Self, the realization of which frees one from suffering. There are many ways to relate to the Self, but I see it as an intimate lover, in whose presence I feel deliciously comfortable. Try surrendering, melting into its compassionate embrace. When the ego opens up to Silence, its cleansing waters flood in, healing body and mind.

The Silence may manifest as peace, the sense of being completely at rest, fulfilled and unconcerned.

Or as bubbling blissfulness.

Or limitlessness, spacious emptiness and fullness.

Contact of the mind with the Self can be described in many ways, but experience of the Self through the mind is not Self-knowledge, enlightenment.

Enlightenment is the rediscovery of oneself as the Self.

The question of what illumines the blissful, silent, peaceful state needs to be answered. How is this Self, which is routinely ignored in the waking state, suddenly available for experience? Is someone other than it illumining it or is it illumining itself? What is the nature of the Self and how does it relate to the "me" I think I am?

The purpose of meditation, working with the breath and mind, is to create an inner environment conducive to the exploration of the Self. As mentioned, most seekers have an exaggerated and fantastic notion of enlightenment. Because their views are so unrealistic, they are not going to get it even when it is staring them straight in the face.

The information necessary to make the discrimination between the Self and the not-Self in meditation is contained in this text. The last chapter contains a list of ideas useful in the inquiry.

Self-Knowledge and Meditation

The best source of knowledge on the Self is scripture, particularly very old texts, the *Upanishads*, for example. These sources, which represent collective knowledge, can be trusted because no specific ego is responsible for them. The experience of contemporary mystics may also be valuable, but only when it squares with scripture. Seek knowledge from many sources and only accept that on which all agree. If someone becomes famous and writes books on meditation, distortions inevitably occur. Forty years ago a *yogi*, whom the author had the pleasure to know, had a profound experience of a "blue pearl" before enlightenment. To this day meditators in his lineage strive to experience it and often feel spiritually dissatisfied when they do not. Extraordinary experiences are not inherently unspiritual, but each path to enlightenment is unique and will only provide experiences relevant to the individual's needs.

Scripture is valuable because the language is impersonal and factual. For example, the following verses from an eighth-century text by Shankaracharya, written in the first person, present the Self as pure knowledge:

> *Negating conditionings with the*
> *knowledge "I am not this,"*
> *realize your identity as the Self*
> *as indicated in scripture.*
> *The three bodies are perceived objects and as perishable as*
> *bubbles.*

Realize through pure discrimination,
I am not them.

Because I am other than the body,
I don't suffer its changes.
I am not born nor do I die.
I have no sense organs,
so I am uninvolved in the world. Because I am other than the
mind,
I am free from sorrow, attachment, malice and fear.
Scripture says I am pure, without thought and desire, and so I am.
I have no attributes.
I live without breath.
I am eternal, formless and ever free.
I am the same in all, filling all things with being. I am infinite,
non-dual, pure Consciousness.

While we can't avoid it, the language of experience can be potentially dangerous. People invariably speak from the point of view of a subject looking out at an object. The objects, one's experiences, are usually the points of interest to them, not the subject, the one who is reporting them. If I see a blazing light without limit, the blazing limitless light captures my attention and will be assumed to be the content of the experience. However, the Consciousness that witnessed the light is the essential ingredient, and the light non-essential, because nothing is experienced without Consciousness. Were the light the Self it would be conscious of being witnessed, but subtle objects of experience, like dreams, are never conscious. Seeing a light or lights is a common experience which should stimulate inquiry. What "light" is illumining the light? Who saw the light? The "who" is you, the Self, whose existence is not validated by a particular experience. In fact without knowledge of what we are seeking the meditator can easily live from experience to experience, craving more and more, building a grotesque, addicted spiritual ego.

So the point of having clear knowledge going into meditation is to arm the meditator with discrimination. Discrimination allows the meditator to skillfully wade through the endless experiential phenomena that take attention away from the Self.[35]

35. See the list of terms in Chapter V describing the nature of the Self.

Meditation as Therapy

Meditation is a means of Self-realization. Realistically, however, Self-realization is at best a distant goal, attainable by the few. Moreover, the authorities insist that Self-realization only comes when the mind is relatively free of neuroses. Since freedom from suffering is everyone's goal, meditation is also psychologically valuable because it acts as a bridge between the conscious and unconscious minds, and brings the causes of suffering to light. When the causes are acknowledged, they dissolve and suffering ceases. Whilst the theory is a little crude, and enlightenment can happen before the *samskaras* are completely exhausted,[36] the idea is sound and provides a reasonable rationale for practicing meditation.

Therapy,[37] because it doesn't introduce the patient to the Self and takes the ego for the Self, can only split the mind into two parts and train one to observe the other. The therapist assumes the position of a dispassionate witness, observing from beyond the dark penumbra cast by the ego, facilitating the exposure of Shadow content. Ideally the therapist's point of view is transferred, and the patient begins seeing objectively.

The science of meditation claims that everyone has a built-in inner therapist, the Self, in whose compassionate light the ego's habits and patterns are objectively revealed. Meditation is not necessarily superior to therapy, but at some point the objective view of oneself has to ironically come from within.

Enlightenment is nothing more than assuming the Self's point of view as one's own. Identification with the Self gives lasting happiness because it frees one of limiting concepts.

Limiting Concepts: The Not-Self

I Am the Body

"I am the body" is our most pervasive and severely limiting concept, and the source of much grief, the immense fear of disease, old age and death, for example. Why am I not the body?

First, because **it is perceivable,** an object of my awareness. I see or feel it, therefore it is other than me. The Self is the perceiver.

---

36. Chapter III describes the techniques for purifying the *samskaras*.

37. See the beginning of Chapter V for more on psychotherapy and meditation.

Second, because **it is insentient.** If I were the body, the body would know me just as I know it, but the body has no idea of who I am. The Self is eternally sentient.

Third, because **it is limited** and **not constantly present.** If I am the body, why do I not exist in the dream and deep sleep state? I do exist in those states, but not as a physical body. Even in the dream state, where I may have a body, the dream body is not the same as the waking state body. If I am two bodies, there are two "me"s, an obvious impossibility. In deep sleep I have neither a gross, waking or subtle dream body, therefore the body isn't me. The Self is unlimited and omnipresent.

Fourth, because **it changes.** The Self doesn't.

Fifth, because **the body has a shape.** The Self is formless being.

Sixth, because **the body depends on its constituent parts and the elements.** The Self is a partless whole and independent of everything.

I Am the Mind

When I am ignored or rejected, my statement "you hurt me" indicates a confusion of the "me," the Self, with the mind. "I am angry, sad, depressed, jealous, envious, etc." are further examples. You are not your feelings and emotions for the same reason you are not the physical body. Feelings and emotions, like the body, are insentient. They do not know you. Because of you they are known.

And like the body, the mind does not exist in all three states. Sleep is only possible when the mind dies, yet you do not cease to exist without the mind.

I Am the Intellect

The third layer of ignorance to be discriminated as not-Self is identification with ideas, thoughts and ideals. "I am a doctor, lawyer, communist, capitalist, Christian, mother, father, gay, black, lesbian, meditator, etc." are spiritually incorrect statements. The "I" is the awareness in whose light all ideas are known. Like the body and emotions, ideas are not conscious.

I Am the Ego

A fourth misconception causes identification of the Self with the ego, the doer and enjoyer; "I climbed a mountain" is untrue. The body climbed the mountain. The "I" watched it climb. "I want a job" is untrue. The ego wants a job.

Like the body, the mind/intellect/ego is a perceived object and limited with respect to experience. Its non-existence in sleep also confirms its relative unreality.

One might argue that if the Self is everything, the body, mind, intellect and ego are the Self, and therefore enlightened by default, just as an effect is the cause in a different form. But the effects of the Self are non-essential with reference to Consciousness and therefore not enlightened. A spider's web, for example, manufactured from the body of the spider is non-separate from the spider with reference to its substance, yet unlike the spider, it lacks consciousness. So until the identification and attachment to the body/mind/intellect is destroyed,[38] enlightenment will not happen.

When the crutches of limiting concepts no longer support the meditator, he or she is forced to stand alone as the Self. The Self, unlike limiting concepts, cannot be discarded.

Try to discard yourself.

Direct experience and knowledge of the Self comes as a surprise because the Self, an intimate but apparently hidden part of every experience, is out in the open. And like one's name, it cannot be forgotten. Meditation is an awakening, a journey without distance, from the state of Self-ignorance to Self-knowledge.

This kind of awakening happens rarely, although there are moments when the Self is known and one could be said to be temporarily enlightened. But owing to factors which will be discussed in the next chapter, the vision fades, the light seemingly goes off and one is returned to the sleepy life of limitation.

38. Conventional wisdom notwithstanding, enlightenment can happen when the meditator is partially identified with the not-Self. It will not come or be momentarily experienced when there is a high degree of identification with the not-Self. Complete identification and non-attachment with the not-Self does not exist on ego's level. Even a highly identified person is capable of moments of meditation and transcendence. Conversely even predominantly non-attached persons are subject to periods of attachment.

CHAPTER II
The Bad News

IF THE PRIMARY purpose of meditation is Self-realization, the rediscovery of oneself as the Self, and if the Self can be realized through meditation and other methods, then why is it so infrequently realized? Why is the spiritual world full of meditators whose underlying sense of inadequacy, incompleteness and limitation remains in spite of innumerable *shaktipats, satoris, nirvanas* and fleeting *samadhis?*[39]

From the ego's point of view life is one long experience broken up into many small experiences. Information comes in from the world around, and it reacts. After enduring a seemingly endless procession of stimuli and an equally countless queue of responses, the lights go out and we die. Stimulus-response is so instinctive, subtle and fleeting that we hardly realize it exists. Deeper analysis, however, reveals a complex and powerful process.

To find out why even seasoned meditators find meditation to be difficult we need to investigate – not the humdrum experiences that pack our daily lives or the peak experiences that flavor them – but the **way** we experience.

Because they steadfastly rely on the senses as their primary means of knowledge,[40] materialists ridicule the view that an externally self-existing, indivisible, non-dual Consciousness, the substrate of material and psychic reality, transforms itself into matter and intelligently divides into five elements, which subsequently split and combine to create the infinite diversity of names and forms that confront our senses. Yet if the ancients are correct, this (or something akin to it) seems to be what happened.

Just as a web is manufactured from a spider's body and shaped by its intelligence, the material world evolved from formless reality, shaped by conscious impersonal intelligence. According to the Vedic view, the Self is not requisitioning matter from a supramundane deity or a parallel universe, but metamorphosing into matter without compromising its formless nature.

---

39. *Shaktipat* is the experience of the inner Self; *satori* a glimpse of the Self. *Nirvana,* a negative description of the Self, means that experience is "blown out," i.e. no longer exists. *Samadhi* is the knowledge that everything one perceives is equal in value to everything else. It is a *yogic* term describing one type of experience of the Self.

40. Those whose primary means of knowledge are the senses tend to think the body is the Self.

The science of the Self, unlike religion, does not ask us to blindly swallow church doctrine or mindlessly take on board unverifiable scriptural contentions – like heaven and hell – but presents time-tested methods that let inquiring meditators verify its theories in the laboratories of their own minds. Its models are not meant to cement profound concepts concerning the precise nature of a given physical or psychological object or process in the mind, but to guide the meditator to practically know the Self, the non-conceptual factor underlying experience. Quaint as it seems, over the centuries the ancient model used to explain the elements' interaction with the senses has provided meditators with a reasonable explanation of an important process, one that aids in understanding the pitfalls inevitably encountered in meditation.

Our discussion of the psychology of meditation begins with the apparently mysterious statement that the sense organs "arise" from the elements.[41] The five elements in order of subtlety are: space, air, fire, water and earth. Their five corresponding properties give rise to the five perceptive senses whose instruments are: ears, skin, eyes, tongue and nose.[42]

For example, the property of space is sound. The Self, Consciousness, accurately labeled the "unstruck sound," is spaceless, and therefore soundless. But Consciousness as matter is dualistic, subject to constant motion. Assuming an ocean of matter, energy in motion, eternally vibrating in limitless space, in turn superimposed on an endless ocean of Consciousness, would it be reckless to speculate that over trillions of years, one day when the elemental mix was just right the first tiny ear emerged from the cosmic soup and began to listen? The ancients say that Consciousness, intelligence, in this or a similar way, developed the power to experience itself in and through matter.

The property of fire is light. The sun, for example, is a massive fire radiating light throughout the solar system. So Consciousness evolved the organ of sight in the Subtle Body and its physical instrument, eyes, to allow itself to visually enjoy its creation.

Air makes the organ of touch and its physical instrument, the skin, possible, allowing us to calculate proximity to physical objects and forces – heat and cold, for example.

The power of taste relies on a tongue immersed in saliva, so water is said to be the source of the organ of taste. A dry tongue tastes nothing.

41. In the diagram on the following page, the upward-moving arrows on the left.

42. In the diagram on the following page, the "Gross Body" in the second column from the left.

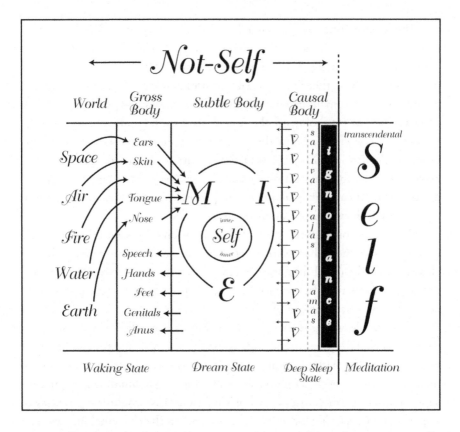

Finally, earth, the densest element, a composite of the others, emits smells, recorded in the subtle body through the nose. The sense instruments (eyes, ears, nose, tongue and skin) are located on the physical body and composed of matter, but the organs proper are located in the subtle body and are formed from the *sattvic*, or light, component of the macrocosmic mind.[43]

So Consciousness has devised a way to "involve" itself into the elements and eventually, when it becomes weary of its game, "evolve" back out of them. The ancients say the elements evolved before the psyche or consciousness,[44] an idea roughly coinciding with the epiphenomenal views of modern science. The idea makes sense if we accept the view that the universe was evolved by the Self

43. See Chapter III for a discussion of the *gunas: sattva, rajas* and *tamas.*

44. Consciousness with a lower-case "c," the subtle body.

45. The middle column of the diagram at the left.

for the purposes of Self-realization because the psyche, or subtle body,[45] would need a field of experience, one capable of providing the experiences necessary to reawaken to its source.

The subtle body, composed of the subtle components of the five elements, molds physical nature to serve its ends. If chemistry is destiny, a predominance of the subtle component of the earth element might lead to a practical nature, the predominance of fire to a passionate temperament, water to emotionality, and air to abstract thought. Moreover, if the ancients are to be believed, a pre-ponderance of a particular subtle element attracts the corresponding physical element into one's body. The permutations and combinations of the elements make for the immense variety of psyches and bodies comprising the creation. Animals and plants are rudimentary subtle bodies interacting with the ele-ments. Air and fire predominate in hummingbirds, for example, while earth and water predominate in hippos.

The relationship between the psyche, the subtle body, and the material world makes experience and knowledge possible. If the creation were exclusive-ly elemental and conscious beings absent, nothing will be known. For example, electricity, as opposed to visible matter, is a form of energy. Though gross, a tungsten filament is nonetheless comprised of subtler particles: protons, neu-trons, mesons, quarks and whatnot. When it flows into the filament, electri-cal energy excites subtle particles, which subsequently excite grosser particles, producing light. Similarly, when the subtle consciousness in the sense organ interacts with gross objects, knowledge (psychic light[46]) is produced.

According to Vedic theory the elements evolved from the subtle to the gross. The most subtle element and first to evolve was space. Because it per-vades everything, is unaffected by what it pervades and is intangible, it is often confused with the Self. In spite of similarities, it can't be the Self, because it is insentient. The invisible container of the other elements, we infer its presence by listening to the sound vibrations arising in it. Sound doesn't exist where there is no space. The Self is silence because it is spaceless. Sound cannot be seen, felt, tasted or smelled. The apparent feeling of sound vibration is due to the skin's contact with air that has been disturbed by sound. Air, the next ele-ment, can be heard through the ears and felt through the organ of touch. The smells in air come from earth particles carried by it, not from the air itself. Fire, the first element perceivable by the physical eyes, can be seen, heard and felt.

---

46. The word "light" in spiritual literature generally refers to Consciousness, the knowing principle, and knowledge, the result of the mind's interaction with objects.

Water, number four, can be seen, heard, touched and tasted. Finally, earth, the element that made noses possible, can be smelled, seen, tasted, felt and heard.

Why, if five separate senses report five different stimuli in five separate theaters, do not conscious beings enjoy five separate simultaneous experiences?

Enter mind, the mixer.

What a marvel! Five unique perceptions involving myriad bits of information combine to create one cogent perception.[47]

So the universal foundation of experience is sense contact with the sense objects, symbolized by the five-element model.

On the way to the supermarket a car ran a stop sign and came hurtling at me. I screamed, slammed on the brakes and turned the wheel, narrowly avoiding an accident. Though such a situation had never before happened to me, why did I react so swiftly and appropriately?

A speeding object emits stimuli which strike my retina. The mind sends a signal to three of my five active organs, and an accident is avoided.[48] How did the mind know what to do?

In fact the mind's command to the senses was the final step in a very subtle process taking place at an even deeper level. Moreover, the mind did not unilaterally make the decision, but merely executed a command coming from a higher center, intellect, the discriminating function.[49]

The mind not only executes instructions coming from intellect but sends the unified sense stimuli garnered in the world up to intellect, which decides how to respond. On the basis of what?

The Causal Body

Imagine this situation: on the first day of creation a mountain shaped like a perfect cone thrust out of the earth, and the first drop of rain struck the mountain's very tip.

What path would the drop take?

---

47. In the diagram on page 42, the five downward-flowing arrows converging on "M."

48. In the diagram on page 42, the five small arrows moving from "E" to the active senses in the second column.

49. In the diagram on page 42, the two large arrows moving from "I" to "E" and "E" to "M."

Since no precedent exists, each potential path is as likely as any other. Let's say it flipped a coin to determine its course and slid down the south side, leaving an imperceptible little trail.

Time passed and a second drop fell. What path would it take? High odds favor all paths, but marginally greater odds favor the south side. It followed tradition and etched the existing path a little deeper. After thousands of rainstorms other paths developed, and the mountain sported canyons, ravines and gullies all around. And the original path became a great river valley.

We obviously cannot go back to the time when our psyches were perfectly clear like the Consciousness from which they emerged, but let us pretend we can. On the day First Mountain sprang up, First Man strolled out of his cave and looked around just as First Bear wandered out from behind the first tree. The bear spied the man and decided to have lunch. The man, however, picked up a huge rock and struck the bear so hard it died instantly. And, in life's first irony, First Man enjoyed the world's first bearburger for lunch.

What kind of a day was it for our hero? Because it was his first experience and he had no others with which to compare it, he could not say. As he sat contentedly munching his burger, the experience replayed several times, gradually diminishing in intensity and frequency. When evening fell it left his consciousness entirely, and he dropped off to sleep.

On the second day First Man bumped into First Woman, one thing led to another and they made the first love, a delightful experience. When he fell asleep after dinner, the memory accompanied him and cooked up delicious dreams.

The next few days saw many experiences, some good, some not so good. One morning, a week later, he woke up, ate his porridge and looked out through the entrance to his cave to see a hungry bear looking in. Suddenly an exciting and emotional replay of the encounter with the first bear flashed in his primitive consciousness and he understood what to expect if he ventured out.

Each experience, no matter how trivial, leaves a trace in our consciousness, like an elementary particle carving a track in a cloud chamber. The deep memory that saves experience, unlike intellect's facts-and-figures memory, is the causal body, the unconscious, which not only retains the essence of each experience but also the subjective reactions to it: the feelings, emotions and thoughts arising in the mind at the time.

What a blessing to have his experiences stored out of consciousness! He could get up in the morning, take his porridge and venture out into the light of day without having the past intrude, very much like the first day.

But as time passed he noticed a change. One day, walking along without a care, he began to feel a little out of sorts, as if he wanted something. Trying to picture what he wanted made him uncomfortable, and he was unable to keep his attention on the pristine world around. Suddenly he knew! A picture of First Woman appeared in his mind and the experience of their tryst vividly flooded his consciousness. Because the memory was so pleasurable and First Woman was no longer available, he became unhappy. He wandered about in this state for several days when, as luck would have it, he met the second woman of the world. To make a long story short, they made love and the first man was happy once more.

After repeatedly cataloguing the love experiences, the causal body realized it was running out of storage space and edited the extraneous details: the color of her hair, the cut of her garment and her name, saving only important facts like the grunts and groans, and (of course) the big moment when the world stopped. As more experience flowed in, it merged the experiences of many different women into the essence of woman, compacted myriad episodes into the essence of love and created a file marked "high priority." Though the memories were meant to remain "sub"-conscious, the woman-memory eventually took on a life of its own, popping into his conscious mind, the subtle body, with disturbing regularity. Moreover, each repeated memory deepened the scar in the pristine landscape of his subconscious until it resembled the great river valley on the side of the first mountain after millions of years of wind and weather.

Now, sadly, when First Man awoke he had an agenda. No longer able to sit blissfully in front of the cave enjoying the scenery as he'd done before, he passed his days longing for a companion. Just as rain tends to flow down the mountain's deepest valleys, our hero's consciousness gushed wildly down the deep sexual groove in the causal body, filling his conscious mind with desire.

His routine changed and he became increasingly indifferent to the practical details of life. Instead of enjoying random walks through the forest, staying home patching cracks in his cave or stocking winter stores, day and night he haunted First Bar hoping to find love. The more he thought about a mate, the more he thought about a mate.

His emotional state was being saved and recycled too. Just obsessing over the memory of love generated great desire. And with each longing the channel in the causal body got deeper and deeper, flooding the mind with fantasies, tossing it hither and thither like a small boat in a storm.

Furthermore, he began to notice a strange connection between his all-consuming desire and the probability of meeting a First-Woman type. Were these the chance encounters they seemed? In the beginning outer life seemed to be creating his inner reality, but now his cravings seemed to control his destiny. Eventually he reached a point where inner reality became as vivid and real as the outer.

We'll leave First Man and return to my drive to the supermarket. Although I'd never been in an accident, I knew exactly how to respond because the causal body, which contains both the personal subconscious (the impressions of personal experience) and the collective unconscious (the impressions of the experience of all beings[50]), stored the memory of that or a similar situation and activated the chain reaction that resulted in an appropriate response to the threatening situation.

In a fraction of a second, intellect, based on information stored in the causal body, determined danger, passed on the information to ego, the top dog of the inner triumvirate, whose identification with the gross body compelled it to instruct mind to generate intense fear and activate the hands and feet, causing the car to swerve and avoid the accident.

The five executive organs, which evolve from the *rajasic*[51] aspect of the macrocosmic mind and correspond to the five information-gathering senses, are: speech, hands, feet, genitals and anus. Speech, which evolves from the active element in space, corresponds to the ears. Hands evolve from the active element in air and correspond to the skin. Feet, corresponding to the eyes, come from fire's active element, and the genitals, born of water's active element, correspond to the tongue. The earth element generates the anus, which corresponds to the nose.

To round out our model, five "vital airs" (respiration, evacuation, circulation, assimilation and *udana*, the power to initiate thought and eject the subtle body from the physical body at the time of death) account for the autonomic processes that keep the physiological systems functioning.

The traces left in the causal body by repeated experience are called *vasanas*, impressions, in Sanskrit. When they accumulate, *vasanas* become *samskaras*, deep channels, and generate a terrible internal pressure which causes life to become neurotic and obsessive. Instead of waiting to see what comes, we frantically try to make things happen by creating favorably, and avoiding unfavorably, remembered experiences. *Samskara* means "formation" and is similar to the psy-

---

50. Often called "instinct."

51. See the discussion of the *gunas* in Chapter III.

chological idea of a "complex," an amalgam of subtle tendencies that produce a particular mental/emotional condition.

Whether life is a spontaneous reaction to external factors, a subjective compulsion to manipulate external factors based on past experience or a combination of the two, attention is always fixed on either the gross or the subtle bodies. **Focusing on these bodies is not meditation. Meditation is the flowing of attention toward the Self – which is even subtler than the causal body.**

The Self is not directly involved in life processes. Just as the sun blesses earthly activities with its radiance but doesn't actively participate in specific activities, the Self simply provides the consciousness that enlivens the gross, subtle and causal bodies. From its point of view, sentient beings are perfectly free to respond to life spontaneously or according to programmed patterns of habit and thought.

Perhaps the most serious obstacle to meditation is the obsession of the subtle body, the instrument of meditation, with happenings in outer reality.

The causal body determines the type and quality of experience, hence the word "causal." No thought, feeling, emotion, memory, fantasy, dream, desire or idea appears in the subtle body that has not sprouted from a causal body seed. Moreover, all physical actions flow from subtle body motivations.

Knowledge of the factors influencing the subtle body is essential because it is the instrument of meditation.

Since most experience is worldly, the typical subtle body is extroverted. However, the causal body indiscriminately saves information, subtle and gross, mystical and worldly, so Self-experience, which often happens spontaneously, creates powerful introverting *samskaras*. Meditation also produces introverting *samskaras*, encouraging the tendency to seek within. Because of the belief that happiness only comes from outside, materialists consider introversion undesirable, but introversion caused by spiritual practice is not incompatible with dynamic work. In fact inner vision, which will not develop properly until one's relationship with the world is satisfactory, enhances outer awareness.

The Subtle Body

Spiritual practice indirectly changes the causal body, which is unmanifest[52] and beyond the conscious control of the subtle body. The following chapter discusses methods other than meditation affecting the causal body.

The instrument of meditation, the subtle body, commonly called the mind, controls the perceptive and active organs, and the vital airs.

The subtle body functions in three capacities: as mind, intellect and ego.[53]

Mind is the "emotional center" in the subtle body, the "feeling function," or the "heart." In its passive aspect it tunes into and plays feelings and emotions like a radio. In its active role it projects a wide array of positive and negative feelings: anger, jealousy, possessiveness, kindness, love, sympathy, affection, etc. Like the senses, which are nervously fixated on the material world, the mind[54] is obsessively riveted on the emotional world, constantly on guard against negative impulses from hostile minds, nervously anticipating tender sympathies from kindred hearts. Identification with and attachment to the mind is one of the primary obstacles to meditation.

The intellect, another subtle body function, is involved in the analysis of situations, inquiry into problems, making determinations and discriminations. Though simply a function like perception, sensation and emotion, intellect plays an important role in spiritual life since suffering and enjoyment are ultimately tied to what we know about ourselves and the world.

In the service of worldly ends, intellect's powers of abstract thought, reason and discrimination render it an obstacle to meditation and spiritual growth. A little subtler than the mind, a bit closer to the Self, the source of its intelligence, it can, if educated and trained to think objectively, become a powerful meditative aid.

Ego and the Inner Enemies

The subtle body's third limb is called ego. No word is bandied about more enthusiastically than ego. What is ego? Is it good or bad? How does it relate to meditation and the Self?

52. The causal body, because it is subtler than our perceiving instruments, the senses, mind and intellect, cannot be directly perceived.

53. The following discussion of the subtle body, like the preceding discussion of the gross body, is simply a model. The idea that the mind, intellect and ego are separate conscious entities is imprecise. They are actually inert feeling/thought bundles that seem conscious because of their association with the Self. Seeing the Self functioning in three modes may be more helpful. The model is meant to assist the meditator in isolating these inner factors in his or her understanding.

54. The word "mind" has many meanings. Describing the emotional function as mind is confusing because the term generally refers to the thinking function. I've retained the Vedic term *manas* (mind) because the *mantras* use a separate term, *buddhi*, to describe the thinking apparatus, the intellect. The mind, or "heart," is not to be confused with either the physical heart or the *hrydaya*, the spiritual "Heart," or Self. As a symbol of the self, "Heart" means "essence," as in the "heart of the matter," because the Self is the essence of everything.

In Vedantic literature the word has several meanings. One defines ego as the part of the Self that thinks it's a doer and/or enjoyer. It identifies with actions, accomplishments, joys and sorrows, the physical world and the body particularly. "I did this, I did that" are egoic statements because the Self is un-embodied and a non-doer.

Two related terms, *jiva* and *ahamkara*, also define ego. A *jiva*, or ego, is an embodied being. Plants, animals, insects, microbes and humans are embodied beings. This definition says nothing about what these egos think about themselves or the world. *Jivas* are sometimes conceived as "rays" or "emanations" of formless Consciousness, "man cast in the image of God," and are apparently separate from Consciousness. *Jivas* are embodied Consciousness and share its essential nature, but seem separate when viewed from their own perspective. When viewed from the Self they are not separate.

Ahamkara is a compound word. *Aham* means "I," and *kara* means a "notion or idea." So *ahamkara* is the notion or idea a *jiva* has about itself. Needless to say, egos who have no notion they're one with the Self have a plethora of ideas about themselves. This more reasonable and helpful definition sees ego not as a flawed individual but as the perfect Self temporarily flawed by an incorrect self-concept – the idea that it is separate from the world, from other beings and from the Self.

When a pure and perfect being seemingly forgets its limitless nature, it un-consciously concocts a secondary identity – the association of an "I" with a long string of apparently related experiences. To compensate for its insecurity in the face of the unstructured oceanic reality of existence, the secondary entity nur-tures a belief in a solid material reality and sees itself as limited by the body and mind. Since billions think of themselves in this way, they reinforce each other's ignorance, therefore little incentive to discover the truth exists in their world.

Because the Self-knowledge arising during inquiry destroys this idea, *ahamkara* is said to be (Self)-ignorance, or egoism. **The ultimate goal of spiritual life is the removal of this ignorance.**

To more completely understand the phenomenon of ego, let us trace its birth and development.[55]

The Separation

If I am limitless, adequate and complete, yet think of myself as limited, inad-equate and incomplete, I am living a lie. Christianity has labeled this separated state "original sin." It is "original" because it is the source of erroneous views about oneself, the world and "God" – the Self. It is called "sin"[56] because it misses the mark about who we really are. To miss the mark is to suffer.

STAGE ONE: GUILT

The error of non-apprehension[57] of the Self is the mother of ego and the cause of a chain of negative states of mind, the first of which is guilt – feeling bad for making a mistake. Guilt, which is largely unconscious and a synonym for the Separation, torments us until we realize what we're missing by living out of the light of the Self. We would like to erase the mistake but have in the interim subconsciously accumulated a great store of negative feelings, beliefs, ideas and experiences which continually roil and cloud the mind with reaction, attachment and delusion. Attached, reactive, deluded minds are incapable of meditation. We infer guilt by observing our self-loathing, anger, depression, inadequacy, failure, impotence, emptiness, longing, desire, arrogance and the constant feeling that things should be more-better-different.

STAGE TWO: FEAR

The psychology of ego is infantile and may account for the religious view of humans as "children" of God. When a child breaks the rules he or she immediately fears punishment. But "God," the Self, being unconditional love, will not punish us for separating but – here's the rub – we believe it will. Perhaps fear is a reasonable reaction to the Separation because we have unwittingly removed our true support and protection in life. The longer we remain separate, the deeper the hidden reservoir of fear becomes. Unfortunately, the causal body is dynamic, and fear oozes out, attaching itself in thousands of ways to various objects, both animate and inanimate, polluting our contact with the world.

55. Although this process has been known since time immemorial, the author is indebted to Kenneth Wapnik for fleshing it out in clear, modern psychological language.

56. Drawn from archery, the word "sin" originally meant "to miss the mark."

57. The greater one's sense of separation from the Self, the more one's actions are motivated by guilt, fear, anger and desire. Because it is unaware of its common identity with the Self, ego develops a relentless and single-pointed drive for success, continually faces the prospect of failure and constantly wars with the world and those parts of itself that seem to limit its freedom. Its inflations and deflations, grandiosity and low self-esteem render it unfit as a stabilizing factor in the psychic economy. Like the mind and intellect, ego is subject to the vagaries of power and may support its fellows one moment and attack them the next.

Stage Three: Denial

The best way to live with fear – mutated guilt – is to repress it, push it down into the causal body, a phenomenon known in the psychological world as denial. However, what goes in must come out, so the repressed energy eventually erupts into the subtle body, creating intense extroverting waves which completely obscure the Self, making meditation quite impossible.

Stage Four: Projection

When guilt erupts, the subtle body is painfully conscious of it. To avoid taking responsibility, the ego quickly and automatically directs the pain to an object. It finds convenient scapegoats: the world, Mom and Pop, its childhood, the government, fate – and even God. The unconscious purpose of projection is to separate the ego from the "sin" of Self-separation, even though Self-separation is not all bad from ego's point of view, because it opens up the fertile field of victimhood – which makes it feel marginally better about itself.

Stage Five: Anger and Attack

Having successfully laid the blame on someone or something outside, the next logical step is: get angry at the object, usually a person, and attack. The need to project guilt is perhaps the major root of hatred and anger. Anger, obviously, is inimical to meditation because attention, instead of flowing inward toward the Self, is completely wrapped up in projected objects.

By following ego's idea we seem to have solved the problem – but attack makes us feel guilty. So instead of doing away with our uncomfortable emotions we are right back where we started. And, as if to make matters worse, the ego, who is no fool, has a vested interest in seeing that we believe in the reality of the Separation. As long as we believe we are separate, ego is in business because it is the belief that we are separate.

So when we take up a spiritual way of life and begin to practice meditation we not only have to contend with ego's self-serving thought system but its predictably negative view of our desire to meditate.

Perhaps the biggest danger on the path of meditation is allowing the ego to co-opt the meditation by donning the guise of a sincere, humble meditator. Meditation practice should facilitate ego transcendence, disengage ego identification and purify the subtle body to the degree that it lifts the mind into the plane of the Self, where the ego is no longer the subject, the experiencer, but "becomes" an object of the Self's awareness. Meditations that fail to expose the ego and ego-generated thoughts and emotions won't lead to Self-knowledge, even if they produce extraordinary experiences.

If we define meditation on the level of practice as purification of the thought and feeling waves in the subtle body, we have our work cut out for us. If we understand meditation as the flow of attention toward the Self, one can easily see how subtle-body disturbance keeps us merely "processing" the effects of our spiritual ignorance instead of meditating on the Self. "Processing" is an ego-driven activity, designed to keep ego firmly in control of thought processes, unlike meditation which should free thoughts and feelings from ego manipulation and control. If **meditation is also the process of undoing the tight knots of the psyche through Self-awareness,** this convoluted psychological mess is what we have to work with.

STAGE SIX: DEFENSE

As if dealing with the guilt-denial-projection-fear-attack cycle were not enough, a secondary complex develops – the attack-defense cycle. When you attack you need armor, a defensive posture, because of the fear of being attacked back. The more we defend ourselves the more we reinforce our guilt. Attack is projected fear, so defense is an attempt to protect against fear, but like all Separation-induced thoughts and feelings, it reinforces the precise *samskara* it is intended to relieve.

If the ultimate purpose of meditation is to provide an environment conducive to inquiry and Self-knowledge, participation in ego's game is a waste of time because it teaches that the guilty, fearful ego is the self.

Desire

Another apparently less pathological obstacle to meditation and inquiry is desire.

The Separation creates a firm belief in scarcity. Poverty, psychological or physical, generates intense need for the possession and enjoyment of objects (things, situations, relationships, feelings, ideas, etc.) which are thought to make one feel complete and erase the sense of limitation and inadequacy. In consumer-oriented cultures probably no belief commands as much sympathy and support as the view of ourselves as needy, wanting creatures.

Wanting Is Suffering

The idea that desire is an inherently unworkable and self-defeating game plan is a remarkably unpopular criticism of ego's thought-and-feeling system. Yet no matter how you wish to see it, wanting is suffering. Still, the ego fanatically worships desire – which it sees as an easy way to resolve its sense of limitation and inadequacy.

That the world is in constant flux is the fly in the ointment of this theory of happiness, however. Even if ego gets what it wants, the object eventually loses attractiveness and the mind changes. Or the mind changes, causing the object to lose attractiveness. Or the relationship between the desirer and the desired breaks down, as relationships are wont to do. Were ego to continually get what it wants, the feeling of poverty would not disappear, because it is produced by ignorance, an unexamined misconception about who the ego really is.

Inner Conflict

As if the picture painted so far were not grim enough, when the mind is not in meditation, the Self unknown and the causal body chock-full of unpurified *samskaras*, over time a structural distortion takes place in the subtle body that becomes a secondary source of conflict – which also mitigates against successful meditation.

As mentioned above, each limb of the subtle body has its own agenda and functions in its own limited way. The mind deals with emotional issues, the intellect with thought life, and the ego attempts to control the way the body, mind and intellect serve or fail to serve its desires.

Seduced by an irrational belief in the reality and supremacy of "feelings," the mind insists that spontaneous emotion will bring happiness, needily seeks love and quickly becomes embroiled in the emotional world where it uses its impressive arsenal of emotions to get what it wants. Mind-dominated egos view the intellect and reality-based advice with suspicion – as an attack on the value of "feelings."

Intellect, the world of ideas, dominates the psychic economy when there is a strong conviction that happiness can be attained through careful analysis, inquiry, logic and reason. Intellectuals live mainly in their heads and often view the emotional side with distrust and suspicion. Rather than discriminate between the Self and the not-Self,[58] the intellect contributes to inner disharmony by questioning ego's every desire and action, developing agendas based

58. Vedanta defines the Separation as "the non-apprehension of reality and the subsequent misapprehensions that arise." Its technical term for the Separation is *maya*, "that which isn't."

58. *Viveka*.

solely on fantasy, inquiring into spiritually useless paths and discriminating between assorted unrealities. When it should be offering impartial counsel, it often plays handmaiden to mind, providing self-serving rationalizations and justifications for the emotional approach or cooking up grandiose schemes to please a needy ego.

The greater one's sense of separation from the Self, the more one's actions are motivated by guilt, fear, anger and desire. Because it is unaware of its common identity with the Self, ego develops a relentless and single-pointed drive for success, continually faces the prospect of failure and constantly wars with the world and those parts of itself that seem to limit its freedom. Its inflations and deflations, grandiosity and low self-esteem render it unfit as a stabilizing factor in the psychic economy. Like the mind and intellect, ego is subject to the vagaries of power and may support its fellows one moment and attack them the next.

Intense and consistent pressure over time from the *samskaras* compromises the subtle body's perfect geometry and contorts the personality to the point where it is incapable of living in a peaceful, dignified and meditative manner.

Depressing as this discussion of the obstacles to meditation may seem, serious meditators need a realistic understanding of what they are up against. The following chapter discusses techniques that make the mind meditation-worthy.

CHAPTER III
The Paths

HOW WE LIVE impacts on meditation practice. If instead of experiencing transcendence you find yourself continually slogging through *samskara*-driven problems, struggling with heavy waves of emotion and striving to suppress unremitting thought projections, a lifestyle calculated to purify extroverting *samskaras* and reprogram the causal body is advised.

Purification

Therefore a program of purification must accompany the practice of meditation. "Pure" means uncontaminated. Substances can be purified in theory, but in practice nothing in nature, the not-Self, exists in a perfectly pure state. The three bodies, for example, are aggregates of the gross and subtle elements. The causal body, the primary obstacle to meditation, draws positive and negative energies from the macrocosmic mind – as well as personal experience – and can never be completely purified. Diligent practice, however, can cleanse it until meditation is effortless, spontaneous and deep. A purified causal body is relatively free of projecting and veiling energies, about which more will be said later in this chapter.

The subtle body can be purified directly or indirectly. Direct purifications are peak experiences and epiphanies which lift the mind and put it in contact with the Self, the "state of meditation." Direct purifications can come through the application of a spiritual or religious techniques, the presence of a spiritually powerful person, the grace of God and unknown causes, positive and negative. A great tide of spiritual energy, *shakti*, rushes like a powerful river into the causal body, spontaneously purging *vasana*-generated thought and emotion, leaving the subtle body still and clear, a perfect mirror in which to identify the Self. Usually unsolicited and the source of great inspiration and faith, spiritual experiences eventually end because powerful unhelpful *vasanas* extrovert the mind again.

Indirect purification, the long-range view, purifies the mind by consciously changing or removing *samskaras*. Unhelpful *vasanas* dominate the mind pictured above, extrovert the attention factor and create disturbing thoughts and feelings that completely obscure the Self. In the mind represented in the following diagram, unhelpful programming has been largely exhausted, causing the centers to turn inward, giving them a constant vision of the Self.

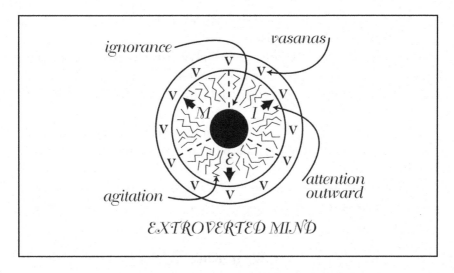

EXTROVERTED MIND

Programming, the *samskaras,* can be helpful or unhelpful. The type of programming is determined by the attitude obtaining when the action that produced the *vasana* was performed. *Samskaras* are helpful when they produce harmonious thought and feeling states, unhelpful when they agitate the subtle

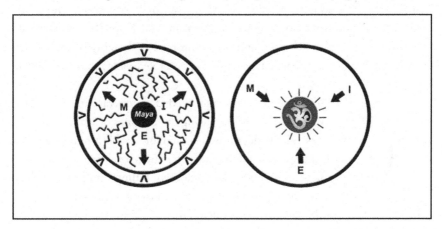

body, extrovert the attention and challenge concentration on subtle objects.

Because I do not know I am the pleasurable Self, I try to get pleasure from a cigarette. Though short-term pleasure may be experienced, the practice is counterproductive because I end up concentrating on the body, reinforcing identification with it and creating a dull state of mind. Smokers can usually meditate only after smoking, when the desire is temporarily submerged. Were a meditative state achieved, it would undoubtedly disappear with the next craving. Additionally, the systematic destruction of the body increases mental and emotional agitation, further reducing awareness.

Actions motivated by selfish craving and excessive concern for results produce unhelpful *vasanas*. For example, if I am unaware that love is my nature I will undoubtedly crave it from others and burden myself with an emotionally disturbed mind.[59]

Fear-motivated actions produce negative *vasanas*. Worry about family, health and money causes even worldly pleasures to be unfulfilling, let alone the bliss of meditation.

Desire-prompted activities produce unhelpful *vasanas*. Greed, pride, lust, deceit – religion's seven deadly sins – extrovert and stir the mind, making it unfit for meditation.

What to Do?

An enjoyed activity produces an attraction *vasana* for that activity. An unenjoyed activity creates an aversion *vasana* for that activity. Without an action, subtle and/or gross, a *vasana* will not be produced. When experience takes place with the mind free of attraction and aversion, no *vasanas* are created. If a course of action is forgone when the *vasana* for it explodes in the subtle body, **the *vasana* does not recycle and is removed from the causal body** – assuming it is acknowledged and not reinforced by longing or repression. Repressed desires come back. Therefore it is possible to add, change or delete *vasanas*.

A person developed colon cancer and needed an operation. The doctor cut the abdomen to remove the cancer, causing the patient's death. Though the operation was unsuccessful, the doctor was lauded for a noble attempt to save a life. Another man walking down a dark alley after the bars closed was accosted by a mugger who thrust a knife into his abdomen, killing him instantly. The robber was vilified and sent to prison for life. The cause of death in both cases, a knife to the gut, was the same, but the killers suffered quite different fates. Were the action inherently evil the doctor would be doing time; were it inherently good the mugger would have gone free. Actions in themselves are neither spiritual nor unspiritual, helpful nor unhelpful, good nor bad. **If the motivating attitude is the critical ingredient in the production of helpful or unhelpful *vasanas*, it stands to reason that changing the nature of the motivation will have an effect on the *vasana*.**

59. See "A Daunting List" in Chapter IV.

Change Your Attitude

To change our attitudes we need to cultivate mindfulness. Mindfulness or self-awareness is constantly compromised because the *vasanas* distract and extrovert attention. Mindfulness is paying attention to and identifying attitudes, especially those which ego prefers to keep in the dark. Altering behavior without changing the underlying attitude does not result in purification and spiritual growth. The action *vasanas* may be obliterated, but not the attitude *vasanas*, leaving a disturbed subtle body. The "dry drunk," an alcoholic who quits drinking but retains the psychology of a drunk, is a case in point.[60]

Attitudes can be binding or non-binding. Binding attitudes produce extroverting *vasanas* and mitigate against meditation.[61] The following attitudes enhance agitating *samskaras*: fear, desire, attachment, pain, guilt, dishonesty, obsession, compulsion, pride, vanity, envy, jealousy, anger, fantasy, delusion, depression, selfishness, concern for results and others.

A non-binding attitude produces a non-binding *vasana* and/or exhausts an existing *vasana*. Non-binding attitudes are: selflessness, compassion (object-motivated love), forgiveness, acceptance, playfulness, dispassion and joy. **Non-binding attitudes are called *yogas*, states of mind that neutralize likes and dislikes, purify the causal body and make the subtle body meditation-worthy.**

Spiritual practice is subtle-body work, attitude adjustment. The three *yogas* purify the three inner centers: action *yoga* purifies ego, love *yoga* purifies mind, and knowledge *yoga* purifies intellect. A purified subtle body is geometrically stable, like an isosceles triangle. No longer under intense pressure from unhelpful *vasanas*, its centers turn inward, fuse together and meditate naturally on the Self. When the causal body has been purified and anxiety for results abandoned, the mind rests comfortably and joyfully in the present, taking what comes with equanimity. The three centers[62] respect each other's turf and cooperate to present a unified front to a changing and uncertain world. In a purified

---

60. Unexamined attitudes keep ego in business. The ego often has a vested interest in maintaining negative *vasanas* even though they cause suffering. For example, individuals with drug or alcohol problems often cling to the habits long after they have ceased to bring pleasure because the attitude associated with the habit brings pleasure – the "poor me" or "victim" mentality – eliciting enough sympathy to partially counteract the suffering caused by the addiction itself. Often just the familiarity of one's feelings causes clinging and prevents self-examination.

61. Addictions and compulsions are extreme examples.

subtle body, intellect, schooled in the knowledge of the Self, cheerfully presents a dispassionate and discriminating view to ego and mind, whose clarity is regularly compromised by emotional passion. Refusing to unduly push a personal agenda, it counsels a balanced response in all situations and, in highly evolved persons, turns its formidable power of observation on itself, ferreting out poorly conceived plans, incorrect analyses and emotion-influenced conclusions.

In the best of all possible inner worlds, mind, ordinarily handmaiden to a needy and selfish ego, resists gratuitous desires,[63] loves purely and faithfully, and refuses to disturb subtle-body equilibrium with petty conceits, insecurities and ill-conceived inflations – while offering support to intellect's well-thought-out *sadhanas*. A well-balanced, satisfied emotional self is a primary qualification for Self-realization.

The tendency to operate exclusively from the emotional center is not conducive to subtle body harmony and causes unnecessary suffering. Because unhealthy emotions are caused by incorrect views about oneself and reality, during initial phases of unrestrained ego-motivated devotion the meditator needs to develop discrimination and dispassion.

The third limb of a purified subtle body, ego, often considered the villain in the piece, should be strong and confident, either because it has successfully negotiated its way through life or because it has the courage to follow its spiritual inclinations. The ego's power needs to come from the realization that happiness lies in serving noble ideals. A mature ego, mindful of its dependence on subjective and objective factors, will carefully heed intellect's counsel, respect mind's feelings and intuitions, refuse to play inner politics and promote inner harmony.

The Path of Action

The ego is the part in each of us that has split from the Self and set up business on its own. A product of Self-ignorance, bedeviled by an unappeaseable emptiness, it is a synonym for desire, the fear-driven power thought to correct

---

62. The three "inner centers" are not actually distinct entities but interconnected functions of the subtle body. And the three "*yogas*" are not wholly independent therapies but interconnected attitudes. The "*yogas*" actually help to break down the artificial barriers between the parts of the inner self, the subtle body.

63. The attempt to repress or deny desire is spiritually counterproductive because the unconscious is extremely powerful and will not be tamed by willpower. The meditator needs to take the long-term view, gradually eliminating gratuitous desires. As the small desires are effaced, the mind becomes more peaceful and confidence builds, allowing one to take on more well-entrenched *vasanas*.

the (unconscious) separation from the Self. Desire implies action, and the ego is a doer, eager to act on the belief that the joy is in the object.[64]

Actions Have Consequences

Prudent individuals consider the consequences of their actions because every action or non-action performed in the field of Consciousness produces specific results that rebound back to the doer. For example, we take employment and a check comes two weeks later. Teeth are brushed so cavities don't develop. However, no matter how seemingly intelligent they are on the surface, the **performance of action solely for intended results is spiritually unwise because attention, which should be concentrated on the skillful performance of the action, is dissipated by anxious concern for results.** Because it is so obsessed with an imagined result, a child on a trip to an amusement park says, "Are we having fun yet, Mommy?" How many job assignments have been hopelessly botched and thoroughly unenjoyed because of performance anxiety? A person suffers through school to get a job, gets the job to support a family, produces the family to enjoy retirement and worries about death throughout retirement. At every stage the fullness of the present is unappreciated because of an unhealthy anxiety about the future. Excessive concern for results casts a gloomy shadow over our lives, agitating the subtle body and denying us the full pleasure of meditation in action.

Meditation in Action

To remedy the situation, perform action for its own sake. Understand possible consequences beforehand, but take your attention away from imagined results and put it into the mindful performance of the action itself. When attention is fully engaged in action, thought or feeling (subtle actions), it enters the moment, transcends the mind and experiences the Self. And truth to tell, a fully enjoyed and efficiently performed action is more likely to materialize an intended result than one deprived of the mind's attention. Finally, action from this "here and now" state breaks the *vasana* for results, purifying the subtle body of pernicious, extroverting waves.

Watch for the Ego

Action *yoga* is a change of attitude toward action. Instead of thinking it has been brought to earth to attain happiness through the possession of objects

64. See "The Limitation of Object Happiness," Chapter I.

and the performance of activities, the ego is encouraged to define life's goal as Self-realization. Action *yoga* does not destroy the ego, remove it from daily life or condemn it to specific religious activities, but corrects its relationship to the body and the world. In the short run, however, because of a perceived threat to the ego, action *yoga* may create disturbance and hinder meditation. In fact action *yoga*, because it produces resistance, is an excellent way to identify ego by coaxing it out from behind its wall of self-serving rationalizations and deceits.

Enough theory. How does it work? First, all actions, even the most insignificant, are dedicated to an altar other than one's own desires – and the results renounced. For example, I want a new automobile. Before trying to manifest the desire, I need to examine my motives. Will the purchase make it easier to pursue my spiritual path? If the present vehicle won't get me to work, and I need work to support myself and take care of obligations (so I have time to meditate), the purchase of a vehicle qualifies as action *yoga*. This technique calls for great integrity because the ego is not above using spiritual ideas to justify unspiritual impulses. A capricious motivation – luxury or status, for example – will conflict with spiritual values, agitate the mind and reinforce unhelpful *samskaras*.

Assuming the reasons are not frivolous, come from a loving, serving state of mind, **consciously dedicate the endeavor to a higher altar. Results dedicated to a higher altar accrue to the altar's account rather than to the ego's. This practice, which is the foundation of spiritual living, teaches how to relate one's ultimate ideal to the practical details of life.** When actions are performed for someone or something other than one's ego, there are no disturbing emotions caused by concern for particular results. Actions dedicated to causes and ideals, especially those fueled by a sense of injustice or unexamined motives, do not necessarily qualify as action *yoga*, because the causes may be the result of group ego – as unreal as one's own.

Count Your Blessings

Dedication at the onset of action should be balanced by an attitude of gratitude when results, positive or negative, accrue. Each life experience, no matter how trivial, is a fructification of previous actions and provides an excellent opportunity for practicing gratitude – even when unwanted results manifest. For example, a man took a flight from New York to San Francisco which was forced to make an emergency landing in Oakland, causing him to miss an important appointment. He could either be upset that he didn't receive the intended result or be happy to be alive. **Taking what comes as a gift neutralizes**

likes and dislikes. Since likes and dislikes are the cornerstone of ego, purifying them purifies ego and makes the mind peaceful. Unhealthy attitudes are easy to identify in a peaceful mind.

Desire Is Stress

One major source of agitation is the ego's belief that the likelihood of a favorable consequence is enhanced by desire for a particular outcome. But if the results of actions were a consequence of desire, everyone who ever bought a lottery ticket would win the lottery. The desire for a particular result plays a bit part in the fructification of results.

The nature of the action, the condition of the field in which the action is initiated, the availability of the intended object and the needs of others vying for the same result ultimately determine the result. Finally, intense desire for an object, because it disturbs the mind, often compromises appropriate and timely action, and mitigates against successfully reaping the intended result.

What Will Be Will Be

With actions consecrated and the desire for the results renounced,[65] the anxiety for the result (stress) that usually accompanies the interval between the initiation of an action and its result does not recycle. Therefore the mind eventually becomes quiet because the ego is stress-free as it goes about its business. Practiced consistently, **action *yoga* slowly chips off *vasana* accretions and lets the meditator enjoy a dynamic life while simultaneously preparing the mind for meditation.**

Occasionally, because ego is excessively identified with a spiritually unhealthy desire, the consecration and renunciation of the fruits of action produces short-term mental turbulence. Addictions and compulsions are examples of encrusted desires or fears which, though inimical to spiritual growth, produce strong subtle-body reactions when we try to work on them. Conversely not every action that makes one temporarily feel good is spiritually beneficial. On the basis of short-term benefits, a seemingly reasonable case can be made for pursuing sense pleasures in that their immediate effect is often a feeling of wholeness and contentment. But sense-pursuit does not qualify as spiritual practice, because it produces binding *vasanas* which bring about attachment to objects and habitual activities.

---

65. The results can't be renounced, because they aren't up to the actor. The renunciation of desire is just a formal way of saying "what will be will be."

In summary, action *yoga*, the foundation of inner work, is a discriminating state of mind that purifies the ego and makes the subtle body fit for meditation. Because it reveals motivations, action *yoga*, which requires constant mindfulness, not only removes anxiety and desire but also exhausts negative states generated at any stage of the separation-guilt-denial-projection-attack-defense cycle – because the consecration of action and the glad acceptance of its results effectively neutralizes or transmutes the original motivation and breaks the *vasana*, clearing the mind and insuring that negativities don't recycle.

The Path of Knowledge

If action *yoga* suggests a change in attitude toward action, **knowledge *yoga* requires a change in the way we think.** Ordinarily, because the intellect is Self-ignorant and under ego's passionate influence, its concepts cause suffering. To right the inner disharmony,[66] knowledge *yoga* aims to detach intellect from ego and train it to identify with and think from the Self. "Thinking from the Self" means that impersonal truth, not personal prejudice, becomes the center of one's thought life, the point from which thoughts originate and to which they return.

Self-ignorance manifests first as a confused and unrealistic thought life, then trickles down to disturb and delude the emotions, eventually contaminating one's contact with the outer world. Because it eliminates incorrect, ignorance-born, ego-centered thoughts, reality-based knowledge produces a harmonious, clear and luminous subtle body, one suited to meditation.

The *yoga* of knowledge relies on intellect's power of discrimination, analysis and inquiry to effect changes. Before charging into the spiritual fray armed with personal opinions, ill-considered ideas, beliefs and superstitions, the meditator will be well-served to make a systematic and dispassionate study of his or her chosen path. A clear understanding of the Self and the nature of enlightenment, the three bodies and states, and the methods of purification removes many obstacles from the path.

This knowledge is not merely "intellectual." Nor is it "intuition" or "guidance" which, like book knowledge, are subject to interpretation and misapplication as they filter through ego's entrenched prejudices, fears and desires. Hopefully, it is carefully and systematically imparted by a compassionate Self-realized teacher skilled in the methods of transmission. The knowledge pre-

66. See Chapter II, "Structural Distortions."

sented in this book, for example, is intended to provide an impersonal frame-work for evaluating issues confronting a meditator.

This path's basic technique is the discrimination between the real and the unreal, the seer and the seen, the subject and the object, the ego and the Self, and is meant to be practiced both in the seat of meditation and in daily life. **The meditator should continually strive to bring his or her thought life in line with experience of the Self garnered in meditation and elsewhere.** For example, if I think there is something wrong with me, that I am unworthy or impure, for example, I need to square this idea with the experience of myself in meditation as a whole and complete being.

Not to put too fine a point on it, for the purposes of inquiry and discrimi-nation, the gross, subtle and causal bodies, and the three states, the "not-Self," need to be negated until identification with and attachment to them is dis-solved. Identification and attachment to the unreal[67] prohibits attachment to and identification with the real. Non-attachment is not merely the intellectual conviction that the states, bodies and objects are unreal, but the experience of freedom arising from the destruction of one's connection to them.

Meditation and Self-knowledge go hand in hand. Transcendence in itself, experience of the Self, is not liberation, because it is subject to change, owing to the power of unpurified *samskaras* to generate *samsaric*[68] experience. However, transcendence reveals the Self and facilitates discrimination, not only during transcendental episodes when it is especially powerful, but later in normal ego states, owing to an increase of knowledge-based faith brought on by the experi-ence.

Self-knowledge arising from discrimination produces transcendence. Like the Ouroboros, the mythical creature that ingests itself, intellect skillfully ap-plying knowledge can gobble subtle-body phenomena so effectively that the waves subside completely, producing transcendence.

"Processing," which is not the practice of knowledge, is designed to interpret experience in terms of ego's thought system. Ego, because its view of life is based solely on conclusions derived from skewed interpretation of experience, colored by likes and dislikes, is incapable of properly practicing knowledge. Inquiry, the practice of knowledge, however, views ego as not-Self, effectively eliminating it as a discriminating factor.

---

67. For an extensive definition of reality, see Chapter VI, Fine Points, "The Importance of a Teacher."

68. Ordinary perception and all its attendant emotional and intellectual misconceptions.

Meditation

Nothing purifies like experience of the Self, which releases a flood of healing, cleansing, spiritual energy into the conscious and unconscious minds. Although most epiphanies wear off in a matter of hours, occasionally days, they produce powerful spiritual *vasanas* which can inspire practice and keep the mind focused on the goal. Practiced diligently, meditation techniques purify the mind because they bring awareness to unholy patterns of thought and feeling. Unhealthy thoughts cannot survive the penetrating light of awareness.

Transcendence does not contradict purification. When the meditator transcends the mind and begins to see from the plane of the Self, the need to "maintain" consciousness dissolves, since the Self is effortless awareness. Knowledge of the mind's patterns and complexes is more accurate from the Self's point of view than is knowledge derived from a witness created out of one part of the mind. Secondly, transcendence breaks attachment to the mind, making it easier to work with it.

Finally, transcendence **accompanied by inquiry** can produce Self-knowledge, the ultimate purifier. In fact the Self-realized meditator understands the futility of trying to clean, fix or comprehend something that ultimately has no reality. To the enlightened, the mind is never a problem, with or without disturbing thoughts.

Transforming the Mind

In addition to the extroverting force of the *samskaras* and the development of ego,[69] three causal-body factors color everyday experience and impact on meditation. No psychological, spiritual or philosophical system, except the Vedic, has articulated this aspect of psychic and cosmic reality so carefully, and English words don't do it justice, so I have retained the Sanskrit terms. Because they evolved before the psyche and gross matter, *sattva*, *rajas* and *tamas* in their causal condition cannot be known by the senses. They can, however, be inferred by observing the quality of our thought, feeling and behavior patterns.

Sattva, *rajas* and *tamas* are called *gunas*,[70] which translates as "ropes" and "qualities." The vaguely pejorative "rope" idea implies that these three energies or qualities bind the Self, Consciousness, to its psychic and physical creations. The Self is always transcendent, but for a technical reason[71] apparently gets caught up in its creations. To free the ever-free Self from its apparent identification with material and psychic reality, knowledge of the *gunas* is extremely

69. See Chapter II.

valuable. The rope metaphor is useful in that it invokes the sense of three inter-weaving strands of energy making up the whole creation.

Sattva

The meaning of "*sattva*" can be divined from its root "*sat*," which means Consciousness and is another name of the Self. *Sattva* is the principle of light or knowledge in the universe. The perceptive senses evolved from the *sattvic* aspect of the creation. The senses beam "light," Consciousness, onto the sense objects, making them known, experienceable. The knowledge of sound, for instance, is possible because the *sattvic* element in the hearing center in the subtle body "illumines" the sounds coming in from the material world.

The subtle body knows what it knows because *sattva's* luminous, reflective quality mirrors Consciousness. The mind's creative functions depend on *sattva*. The physical body is least prone to disease when *sattva* predominates because it allows the healing waters of Consciousness to wash away blockages in the physiological systems, purify the nerve channels and invigorate cellular life. When the mind is *sattvic*, clarity of thought occurs, insight is commonplace, intuition active, discrimination precise, dispassion profound and meditation possible. *Sattva* is responsible for intelligence. A mind under its influence is capable of long flights into subtle realms. All occasions of vast knowing and deep understanding depend on *sattva*. It causes happiness because it reflects the bliss of the Self. A happy mind is conducive to meditation and inquiry.

Rajas

To make a pot, clay, an idea in the potter's mind and the energy to shape the clay are necessary. *Sattva* supplies the idea behind the creation, *tamas* the physical substance, and *rajas*[72] the energy needed to mold it. Atomic power, thermodynamics, volcanic activity, the movement of the seas and winds, the physiological and nervous systems and the power to move the mind and emotions are caused by *rajas*. Wherever there is activity, *rajas* is at work. The five physiological systems and the five active organs evolve from *rajas*.

70. Pronounced "goon-uhs."

71. *Maya,* the non-apprehension of the Self.

72. *Vikshepa shakti.*

Psychologically, *rajas* whips the mind into frenzied waves like a strong wind, distorting perception and knowledge. Highly prized by goal-oriented persons, coffee-drinkers especially, for its power to temporarily activate the mind, *rajasic* projections nonetheless reverberate in the subtle body, creating confusion, eventually delusion and ultimately loss of discrimination.

Rajas, the "projecting power," is called the "mode of passion." The conviction that active pursuit of one's goals is the wisest way to deal with uncomfortable feelings of incompleteness and inadequacy is caused by *rajas*. Because of its fiery nature, *rajas* purifies the water elements from the subtle and physical bodies, producing feelings of thirst and attachment. Those suffering from excess *rajas* tend to be emotionally needy and mentally distressed, forced into a life of unceasing activity in an attempt to possess and acquire what is yet to be gained and to protect and insure what has. *Rajas* creates continual static in the mind, which efficiently drains energy, producing dullness.

In spite of motivational benefits, a mind dominated by *rajas* is a powerful enemy because its intense projections – greed, aggression, desire, restlessness, anxiety and longing – obscure the shining of the Self, the true source of peace and happiness. Extroverted *rajasic* people are continually embroiled in conflict because this *guna* forces them to project subconscious content on the world around. As a result they suffer problematic relationships, have little contact with their true feelings and lack Self-knowledge.

Tamas

Tamas, the dark strand in the psychic rope, is known as the "veiling" energy.[73] *Tamas* produces a cloud in the subtle body that hides the Self. Because the Self's loving light cannot break through, the individual lives in spiritual darkness. Fear is a natural reaction to the dark, and when we are fearful we hide, so *tamasic* people hide from themselves, the world and God. The best way to hide is to sleep. So sleep, including all its waking forms, sensual indulgence and the like, is pursued vigorously by those in whom this *guna* predominates. Sleep is a symbol for ignorance, and *tamasic* persons are ignorant of the Self, themselves and goings-on in the world.

Tamas, all that is dark and heavy in nature, is the power of inertia and entropy inherent in things. Physical substance, solidity, substantiality and insentience evolve from *tamas*. An indispensable force, it is responsible for the most

---

73. *Avaranna shakti.*

universally loved and necessary activity – sleep. Without it the mind would never rest and the organism would die.

On a psychological level, moderate *tamas* confers a practical intelligence, but excessive *tamas* causes dullness, inadvertence, lethargy and depression. Just as *rajas* is responsible for the tendency to project, *tamas* is responsible for denial. When the mind rests under its delusory fog, the meditator is incapable of discriminating between the Self and the not-Self, and holding the mind on the Silence.

Tamas can be blamed for the proclivity to escape duties and responsibilities. It discourages ambitious undertakings. A *tamasic* person often leads a sensuous, inadvertent and miserable life, one plagued by accidents, losses and mistakes. Too much *tamas* in the subtle body creates conditions conducive to disease because it blocks the flow of *shakti*, the energizing and healing power of the Self, to the cellular level.

When the *gunas* are balanced, the body and mind are healthy, and the soul relatively happy. Unfortunately, the *gunas* are in a state of continual flux. One predominates for a few hours, then a second and finally a third so that throughout the day one may experience intense activity, moments of clarity and mind-numbing dullness.

Experience has demonstrated a direct connection between mental and emotional pain and a predominance of *rajas* and *tamas* relative to *sattva*. **Meditation and inquiry are only possible in a *sattvic* mind.**

Three buckets of water stand in front of a white wall. The sun reflects off the water, producing three reflected suns on the wall. A strong wind roiling the contents of the first bucket produces a dancing image of the sun. The second, filled with muddy water, produces a dull, dark spot. The third, containing clear and still water, generates an accurate reflection of the sun. If the purpose of meditation is Self-realization and the mind is the instrument through which the Self is known, it stands to reason that accurate identification of the Self depends on a clear still mind.

Pure Mind

When the subtle body is pure, the bliss of the Self uplifts the emotions and awakens subtle devotional feelings. When the subtle body is pure, the Self illumines the intellect, enhancing discrimination and inspiring brilliant thinking. Radiant health results when a *sattvic* subtle body channels the Self's healing energy to the body.

If the meditator consistently feels a sense of uncaused happiness and unexplained peace, the mind is pure. When happiness can't be attributed to a specific situation, change in status, person or persons, belief or belief system and the presence or absence of any object, the mind is pure. A pure mind is free of the belief in attainment and accomplishment. It no longer panders to desire, knows what's happening and is capable of making rational decisions – because *rajas* and *tamas* are controlled. Finally, spontaneous and deep meditations happen automatically or are produced with minimum effort.

Therefore whether one pursues worldly goals or practices meditation for Self-realization, mental peace or health a *sattvic* mind is useful. Complete purification of *rajas* and *tamas* is neither possible nor desirable. Some *tamas* is necessary for grounding experience, both worldly and spiritual, and *rajas* provides the resolve and vitality necessary for purification. But cultivating a pure mind is the primary purpose of spiritual practice.

Therapy and Purification[74]

Modern psychology generally tries to explain suffering with reference to events in the past, childhood particularly, the idea being that parental behavior, abuse (*rajas*) or neglect (*tamas*), produces long-lasting psychological effects. Whilst the idea that "recovering" and "processing" these unhappy experiences can alleviate suffering is well-intentioned and perhaps partially effective, its premise that the ego is the self is reinforced by these practices and will not solve the problem of incompleteness and inadequacy.

Irrespective of past experience, suffering and attachment to negative memories ultimately stems from the inability to attach to the permanent source of happiness within. People with perfectly happy childhoods often suffer as much or more than those with unhappy childhoods, while many with miserable childhoods live happy, productive lives. In other words, **we actually suffer because we have incorrectly identified the self as the ego.** *Tamas* and *rajas* thicken the wall of non-apprehension separating us from the Self and depriving us of our innate happiness.

Seeing the problem this way depersonalizes our view of suffering, thus freeing us, our families and the past of blame. Since what has happened has happened, affixing blame and taking it personally only compounds the problem and requires an additional and difficult step – forgiveness. But if the *gunas* are at fault and can be purified, suffering can be gradually eliminated.

---

74. For more on this topic, see Chapter V.

Spiritual practice doesn't attempt to correct the past or change our circumstances, but to change the way we see ourselves and the world. Directing attention to the highest in us cleanses subconscious sources of pain and minimizes the danger of building a suffering-based identity. If the ego is thought to be the self, its negativities will never be eliminated, because its very existence is a negativity based on a fundamental error. Like therapy, purifying *rajas* and *tamas* will not remove the fundamental error, but it will create conditions suitable for its removal through Self-inquiry, meditation and teaching.

Diet and Lifestyle

The idea of purification needs to extend to all areas of life – social, financial and sexual. One should associate with people who are seriously committed to spiritual growth. Association with worldly people and insincere spiritual types only increases worldliness and reinforces doubts about oneself. Money should be used to create a lifestyle conducive to Self-inquiry. Sexual attitudes and practices, which should be rigorously questioned, need to support rather than conflict with a purification lifestyle.

Because the materials in food that enters our bodies affect the nature of the mind, spiritual culture has evolved a comprehensive science of diet based on the *gunas* and the four elements. The diet is scientific in the sense that optimum health and a meditative intelligence can be partially achieved by experimentally adjusting the relative proportions of *sattva*, *rajas* and *tamas* in the food consumed.

A heavy *tamasic* diet is counterproductive because it creates sleepy waves in the mind. Foods in which the earth element predominates require a greater expenditure of energy to digest, assimilate and excrete, and are considered *tamasic*. With reference to vegetables and grains, for example, eating flesh is considered *tamasic*, although some flesh is relatively *sattvic*, fish and chicken, for example, while others, beef and pork, because they are difficult to purify, are *tamasic*.

The food's form can cause it to be *sattvic* or *tamasic*. For example, cheese is remarkably *tamasic* because it produces sticky mucus which attracts and absorbs environmental toxins and the waste of putrefactive bacteria. In the slow-moving intestinal environment, it bakes encapsulated toxins onto the colon wall, reducing the power of the body to purify itself, slowing all physiological processes. When the physiological processes slow, the brain eventually becomes bogged down and the mind clouds, making meditation difficult. Yogurt in reasonable quantities, on the other hand, though producing mucus, is classified as *sattvic* because it contains enough of the water element to purify easily and consists of beneficial lactobacteria, vitamins and minerals, so it is classified as *sattvic* when ingested in reasonable quantities.

Methods of preparation also impact on the quality of the food. A potato, for instance, in its natural state, is a nice blend of *sattva* and *tamas*. Fry it in animal fat, cover it with butter and sour cream, eat it in large quantities and it becomes decidedly *tamasic*. Broiled steak is less *tamasic* than when fried.

Eat Life

Food should be eaten fresh. Food is not only physical substance but *shakti*, or energy, a manifestation of Consciousness in living beings. An apple plucked from the tree on a cool fall day and eaten immediately is much more spiritually beneficial than one shipped from South America, stored in a refrigerator for months and eaten after a week's stay in a supermarket. The more a food is heated and mixed with other foods, the less *sattvic* it becomes. Food cooked in complex sauces and mixtures of spices places undue stress on the digestive fires, increasing *rajas* in the short run and *tamas* overall. Raw, fibrous foods are exceedingly *sattvic* because they supply clean nutritious energy and absorb toxins on their way through the digestive tract.

Since *tamas* makes flesh, it should be carefully balanced with *rajas* and *sattva* to create the desired body. A Sumo wrestler obviously prizes *tamas*, while a ballerina eschews it, opting instead for a predominance of *rajas* and *sattva*. A meditation lifestyle demands a large percentage of *sattva* and smaller proportions of *rajas* and *tamas*. Creative life-styles that involve much thinking favor larger proportions of *sattva*, lesser proportions of *rajas* and minimal *tamas*.

Rajas, the activity principle, is also found in food. Although many bitter and astringent foods are classified as *rajasic*, the most common and popular *rajasic* food is coffee, prized for its ability to prod the mind into action. Coffee and other stimulants are not recommended, not only because they artificially activate the mind by stimulating the nerves, but because they produce *tamas* post-digestively. Sugar, which gives bursts of *rajasic* energy in the short run, becomes *tamasic* as it passes through the system. The depressed state following the consumption of processed sugar indicates a *tamasic* condition of mind. When the body-mind has been activated by alcohol[75] and other stimulants in which the fire element predominates, for example, so much stress is put on the

---

75. The American Indians appropriately called alcohol "firewater" because of its *rajasic* properties. The post-digestive effect of alcohol is *tamasic*, however, because it turns to sugar in the system.

physiology that the mind is called on to supply the required energy. Not understanding the cause, the ego consumes more *rajas*, often in the form of exciting emotions, which temporarily reactivates the mind but eventually exhausts the system, thereby producing *tamas*. A mind continually required to adjust to the *rajas-tamas* cycle is unfit for meditation.

The sleep-coffee-cigarette *vasana* neatly illustrates the incestuous relationship between *rajas* and *tamas*. When we awaken in the morning feeling *tamasic*, we immediately take a cup of coffee to stimulate the nervous system and activate the mind in order to deal with the world. When the mind starts to sag, another cup is consumed. The effect of coffee, which purifies slowly from the system, is a hyperactive mind. To solve the hyperactivity problem and ground the mind, cigarettes, drugs or other *tamasic* foods are used. And when the dullness makes life inefficient and painful, one seeks a cup of coffee or other stimulants and excitements.

Operating the physiological systems takes energy. If the diet drains energy, then the shortfall must be met by the mind. If the mind is continually drawing on its reserves to adjust the physiological systems, little energy will be available for meditation. A *sattvic* diet of easily digestible and effortlessly excretable high-energy foods purifies the physiological systems, freeing the mind of extra duty.

Adjusting the three *gunas* to purify the mind conserves energy and produces psychic heat. The practice of spending energy as fast or faster than it accumulates, building a large deficit, is not recommended for meditators. A meditator needs sustained, clear energy to restrain the mind from roaming in the past and future while dissipating through the senses. **When the energy builds to a certain level, it self-ignites and becomes a raging fire which feeds on the *vasana* fuel pouring in from the causal body, incinerating the *samskaras* to ash.**[76]

Because each body is a unique combination of elements, the effect of a food should be evaluated by the way the subtle body reacts to it. A couple of beers will put a *sattvic* mind to sleep, but might temporarily quiet a *rajasic* mind. A steady diet of highly spiced food will cause short-term *rajasic* and long-term *tamasic* reactions because spices accumulate in the organs and are difficult to purify. Any high-fiber diet will have a *sattvic* effect on the whole organism.

Purification of the body depends on knowing how the elements work. Fire and water purify the earth element. Air can be used to control the fire element.

---

76. Meditation in India is called *tapas*, "heat-producing," for this reason.

For example, if the mind is too active, regulating the breath can bring it to clarity. If the body is heavy, cardiovascular exercise increases the air element in the blood, activating metabolism (*rajas*) and consuming excess fat. When a particularly dull state clouds the mind, an increase of air can fan the fire of *rajas* and burn off the clouds. The water and air elements are especially helpful in controlling the digestive fires. Water should be consumed in a pure state, uncontaminated with sugars and other pollutants. When the desire for coffee, tea, milk and soft drinks arises, the body is actually asking only for water. The addition of caffeine, sugar and other "tastes" are basically psychological and do not contribute to overall health. Sugars, for example, in their refined state are useless. Taken in the form of fresh fruit, however, they provide clean-burning, efficient fuel. Pure water, uncontaminated by sugars and stimulants, collects rather than deposits contaminants as it passes through the body.

"Eat to live, not live to eat" is the motto of the meditator. The *vasanas* for taste should be carefully examined to determine if cravings are psychological or biological, a difficult discrimination, since attachment to food is a major subtle-body disturbance. Very often parents use food, particularly sugars and fats, to control the emotional states of children, creating an association between happiness and unhealthy *tamasic* food. When a meditator moves to a *sattvic* diet, the fear of unpalatable "tastes" often proves to be an obstacle. As the *samskaras* for particular tastes purify, however, the mind develops an affinity for plain, non-sexy foods.

Study of the stool corrects the diet. Hard, compacted, slow-moving, malodorous stool indicates a *tamasic* diet. Loose, scattered, irregular, multi-textured, multi-colored, fast-moving stool suggests *rajas*. *Sattvic* stool is light, soft, well-formed and not unpleasant to smell.

Finally, although *rajas* and *tamas* are desirable in moderate amounts, the state of mind in which food is gathered, prepared and consumed should be *sattvic*. Because food is given by God to sustain life, one eats with gratitude, not fear or desire. See the body as a temple or an instrument of the Divine and treat it with great love and respect. If the ultimate purpose of life is the realization of the Self and meditation the means to it, then one's relationship to food is important because it directly affects the quality of the mind.

The meditator's physical surroundings should express the *sattvic* principles of beauty and simplicity. Environments loaded with possessions, stimulations and conveniences incarnate activity and dullness, mitigating against clear thinking and peaceful living.

The media, television in particular, and its relentless promotion of excitement, pleasure, convenience, consumption, aggression and body consciousness should be eschewed. Sex without love practiced merely for stress relief or pleasure serves to etch and reinforce deep sensuous *samskaras* in the causal body. On the other hand, pure love, occasionally culminating in sex, integrates the mind.

Become aware of the positive and negative effects of all sources of consumption, gross and subtle. Jettison objects and activities that consistently agitate or dull the mind. Discreetly terminate the relationships with dull and disturbed people unless your presence causes them to begin the process of self-examination. Helping sentient beings on their paths contributes to the universal good and to the *sattvic* condition of one's own mind. Practices like prayer, meditation and selfless service, and relationships with committed meditators and highly evolved beings should be cultivated. To develop *sattva* one follows the "less is more" maxim. The less we require ourselves to deal with material and social reality the more aware and balanced our minds become.

The three-*guna*, four-element model helps diagnose the causes of an extroverted and dull mind, and provides a practical formula for purging *vasanas* and correcting extroversion, thereby making the subtle body meditation-worthy.

CHAPTER IV
The Path *of* Love

ALL HUMAN LONGINGS begin with the Separation without which we would all be wildly happy, children sporting in a garden of delights. Philosophers debate the "why" forever, but we are not concerned with "whys." We simply want it to end. So we search from womb to tomb trying to find the Self we have seemingly lost, the state of pure Love.

We try to find it by falling in love. The love into which we "fall" is very much like the love we are seeking. In it we feel whole, complete, happy, peaceful, powerful, tender, immortal and free. Would that it, like the Love of which it is a pale reflection, last forever.

What is this "in love" love?

Generally Ill-Considered Facts About Emotional Love

Love has to "happen." We cannot just decide willy-nilly to go out and fall in love, because it is a reaction to the deep unconscious need to love (and hopefully be loved), motivated by the Separation. Ignorance of the real reason causes us to make incorrect assumptions concerning the nature and source of the love we are experiencing.

First, though love is our innermost nature and independent of anyone or anything external, we assume it takes two. That it is our nature is demonstrated by the fact that everyone, even rascals, love someone or something. "What's the fuss?" said Mrs. Hun. "Atilla's really a great family man. And he loves his work." Secondly, when love is seemingly absent, we are continually, often frantically, trying to find it. We hang on for dear life when it finds us and sink into the Slough of Despond when it dies.

IDENTIFICATION

"Not knowing it's me – when it happens – I assume it's you. So I fall in love with you. Bathed in the halo of my projection, you seem absolutely wonderful, my white knight. You saved me from my loneliness. Unlike anyone, including my most recent incredible being, the last in a long line (who had the temerity to change and force me not to love him anymore), you are so special, the very best. You have everything I lack. You're funny, I'm serious. You're strong, I'm weak. You're beautiful, I'm plain. In an inexplicable way I see myself in you. I identify so much that even your worn, skin-tight jeans, that old floppy hat you picked up at a garage sale and your snappy little red sports car have become my sacerdotal objects.

"Honesty, however, forces me to admit that even though you are so fantastic certain things about you need fixing. So I'm prepared to set you straight and see that this oneness we feel is absolute. From now on we'll listen to the same music, speak alike, eat the same foods and even dress the same. After twenty or thirty years we should hopefully come to physically resemble each other, like the neighbor and his dog. Wouldn't that be nice?   How I wish I knew when it happened that I was really only in love with me."

I Want to Know All About You

"But wait a minute! Falling in love means, in spite of the wonderfully free feeling of love, that my happiness depends on you. I'm so heavily invested I'm hopelessly attached and can't stand you out of my sight. I live in constant fear of losing you. When you're gone I think of you all the time, imagine what you might be doing, what you're thinking. To protect myself I need to know all your personal secrets, find out what you saw in all those other (horrid) women. It's only sensible that I compare your words and deeds for discrepancies, pry into your past, psychoanalyze you to your face and see that you account for every minute. Can't be too careful, now, can I?

"But oddly, in spite of all this surveillance, I never seem to know what's going on with you. You're as much a mystery as the day we met. Women are from Venus, men from Mars."

Attachment and Anxiety

"I hadn't figured I'd become so clingy when I fell in love. I seem to have been tricked (by you) into thinking I can't do without you, my catalyst, my Cupid. Remember, you shot the arrow. In the old days our love was so terribly free and happy. I even let you do little things on your own and didn't feel jealous at all. But now for some odd reason the more I love you the less I seem to love myself. I'm forever wondering if I'm good enough for you.

"What a terrible irony! In the beginning I loved me more because you made me feel so free. When I think about it I'd have been happier falling in love with me because there's nothing wrong with me and I'm always here, available to be loved. But you, you're much more difficult, always running off to who knows where.

"Not only did I lose my freedom when I fell for you, I got anxiety as a way of life. They say anxiety is reasonable because the world is always changing. I change, you change, the relationship between us changes. Much as I hate to face it, I know, in the back of my mind, that one day we'll no longer be an item (because you've changed). But nothing's to be done, because I'm still in love with you, my ball and chain."

SERVICE AND SURRENDER

"Okay, okay, you're right, it isn't all that bad. Because I love you I want to please you. Your happiness is my happiness. So I'm continually thinking of little things to make your day. Of course this attachment to your happiness has its downside. If you don't feel good, I don't feel good. Why can't I see that you're responsible for your own happiness? And also, why am I neglecting my own needs to satisfy yours? Better yet, why aren't you taking care of me like I'm taking care of you? You go blithely about your business and I go blithely about your business. It doesn't seem right. If love is its own reward, why do I feel so incomplete?

"Along with this desire to serve, I surrender to you, do what you want, an inspired idea that seems okay with you, not my will but thine. This idea, which is terribly romantic, puts me in hot water with my ego, who sees it differently. It would like you to surrender to me, do things my way, since I love you so much."

DESIRE FOR UNION

"Finally, though you're never out of my sight physically or mentally and it's clear you're here to stay, I seem to always "want" you. When you sit down after dinner in front of the TV, I want you here with me, tidying up the kitchen. When you're off on business, the long phone calls are a poor substitute for the real you. I want union. When we make love, I feel unhappy if our special moments are not perfectly synchronized. I won't rest until we're absolutely one. Yet in spite of all our passionate unions, I still feel separate."

THE SLIPPERY SLOPE

"No matter what I do, no matter how hard I try to set you straight, the record speaks for itself. You don't really love me. We never spend quality time together anymore, go out dancing like when we met. You're always schmoozing clients on weekends, working late, watching football even Monday nights. And I know I shouldn't say this, but you've really slacked off in the hay too. You used to take your time, make me feel wonderful. Not anymore. It's all over in a matter of minutes. What's wrong with you? I don't think you love me in spite of all my devotion. The more I think about it the more it seems that you probably never loved me at all. How could you let me love you like that, take advantage of me, vulnerable as I was? It's unconscionable! You beast! You liar! You said you loved me, but we can see what kind of love it really was!

"Well, I've got news for you. I never loved you either. I only loved you for the happiness you brought. I had to work very hard ignoring the many signs cropping up every day telling me you're not my Prince Charming: your bad manners, your vanity, your big ego.

"Just hurt? Defensive? How dare you! I've never been so offended in my whole life! I try to share my feelings with you and this is how you react!

"Okay, maybe it isn't as bad as I make it sound, but believe me, I've had it. Nonetheless, just to show you how lucky you are and because I'm not quite ready to hit the bars looking for my next most incredible someone, for your sake I'm going to dig deep into my magic bag and trundle out another energy-draining psychological trick. I'm going to deny that you're the mess you are and try to see your good side. After all, you pay the bills, make me look good in public and of course we have the whole past-life thing to work out properly, lessons to learn and all that.

"You're worth one more try. I really mean it this time. What? That's baloney! I can do without you. You think I'm some sort of love-starved waif? Over the hill? How dare you! I've never been so offended in my whole life! I've still got my figure, unlike you sitting around all day swilling brew, munching chips! You're wrong, I'm staying for you, giving you one more chance to shape up. Still, I have to admit, every day you're looking more and more like my worst nightmare.

"Here's the plan. We just have too many issues to sort out on our own. We'll do this right, make a proper profession of our relationship, call in the experts. Maybe if you hear it from someone else you'll realize how lucky you are, how much you really do love me down deep. But until I see concrete evidence of your love I'm cutting you off, throwing out my sexy underwear."

HATE

"I was right, you S.O.B. You never loved me. Don't give me that psychobabble you picked up from the shrink. Yes, those are the papers. I get the house, the kids and half your retirement. This is war, you bastard. The best years of my life down the drain."

A Daunting List

As much as we would like to think it is not really like that, it is. And if we are going to sincerely address the emotional side of our personalities, which, sadly, is often the only side, we need to honestly evaluate the importance we give to the idea of love relationships.

Relationship with unexamined motives, not relationship itself, presents a formidable spiritual problem. However, buttressed with the belief that each is responsible for his or her own happiness, relationship or not, and a deep commitment to practicing a higher kind of love, the meditator may find relationships a useful vehicle for attaining spiritual goals.

Nonetheless, before we can develop successful love relationships we should have a clear idea of the psychology of conditional love because the feelings and emotions that confront us in special love relationships are often a neon sign advertising a flawed understanding of ourselves and the world. If we are going to haul our feelings and emotions out of the dark ages and present a pure heart to God, we need to be mindful of the distinction between conditional and unconditional love.

In the first place, I would not need a special love relationship if I were already happy. When I am whole, I feel love. Therefore wholeness equals love. Conversely when I feel incomplete, I crave love. Tormented by the joyful memory of love, I long to be whole again. Because I am cut off, I blame myself and feel guilty, a nasty feeling that spawns a raft of negative emotions, not the least of which is self-loathing. To compensate and reconnect to my most important part, my Self, I unconsciously project love onto someone else and invest my love object with godlike qualities that compensate for things apparently lacking in myself.[77]

Because I am now unconsciously back in touch, in the flush of love, I want to serve, surrender to and know all about my beloved. And to keep love flowing I insist my god or goddess prove his or her love by fulfilling the special needs sprouting like weeds in the fertile field of my incompleteness. My many needs make me dependent and I become attached. The fear that my needs will not be met spawns anxiety and anger.

Unfortunately, the cooperation of my significant other is required to keep this projection alive. But sadly, others seem more concerned with their own needs. So I do not get satisfaction unless I agree to support the beloved's projection by fulfilling his or her special needs – a heavy price to pay. But what to do? If I do not take care of the beloved, he or she will not love me. And I need love because I don't have a clue who I am. Even in the best of all possible worlds

77. See Chapter I, "Removing the Wall."

the love object cannot completely take care of all my needs, and cracks appear in my godlike projection.

To protect myself I need to deny I am projecting and become delusional, which allows me to imagine something's "wrong" with the love object and therefore justify my anger. Anger is psychic aggression and causes guilt, which leads to fear because my angry attacks invite retaliation. To protect myself I need a strong psychic defense mechanism.

Keeping the illusion alive for extended periods is virtually impossible because this type of love is based on ever-changing special needs. Additionally, my relationship to my needs is always changing. To make matters worse, the love object's special needs and relationship to his or her special needs is also always changing. When anger and guilt no longer work, love withers on the vine and, depending on the depth of attachment to my projection (how guilty I am), turns to hate. When I'm sure my love object has failed me, I become disillusioned and bitter, and set out to find a more cooperative victim.

This daunting list of negative psychological effects flowing from the uninformed attempt to heal the Separation by falling[78] in love hardly inspires confidence in the idea of romantic love. Yet falling in love is a universal reaction to the Separation.

Why I'm Fooled by Love

Why does this unlimited unconditional reservoir of love that I am seem to come from outside, to depend on the love object? Because the erroneous belief that I need love extroverts my mind to such a degree I do not realize what is actually happening when I fall in love. This extrovertedness acts as a high barrier, prohibiting access to my innermost Self, the source of love.

The more I'm deprived of love, the more I desire it. And the more I desire it, the thicker the wall becomes. When Cupid shoots the arrow, which is just my desire reaching critical mass, and the object magically appears, the dam collapses and the ocean of love that is my Heart floods into my mind, overwhelming it with happiness.[79]

And, oddly enough, you just "happen" to be there in front of me at the time. Is it any wonder I innocently associate my happiness with you? I am so happy,

---

78. Is this why we use the word "falling" to describe romantic love?

79. See Chapter I, "Removing the Wall."

I not only love you, I love me for being in love, and the world, which heretofore was such a dreary place, does not look too bad either. At least for a while.

Seek Within

After numerous unthinking excursions through this painful psychological landscape, I have enough information to know that "in love" with all its turbulent self-deceptions and disappointments is not real. At the same time the experience of love was real. Something that feels so good has to be real. So even though I reject the "Mr. Right" or "Ms. Right" idea and eschew the magic of "chemistry," I do not let go of the idea that love is what I want. And let us assume that, for whatever reason, I have come to believe the love I am seeking is within me. If so, how would I go about finding it?

Just as we cannot meditate on something we don't know, we cannot love something we do not know. However, though the love that I am permeates everything, I find staying in touch difficult. So I need a path that will convert my many relationships into a spiritual path, one that will bring me in contact with the Self, pure Love.

See God in Everyone

To purify the mind of the ugly *samskaras* listed above and attain union with the Self in love is the purpose of the path of love, the third of four basic approaches to happiness.[80]

The simplest way to accomplish this is to see God in everyone. What is God? God is a symbol for pure Love. I need a symbol because it can't be directly perceived in my present gross state of consciousness. And since I need someone to love, I need to personify Love as God or a god. Personification is an indispensable step on the path of love because the heart thinks in terms of people. Ultimately, when we have worshipped our god of Love for an appropriate time, the heart becomes subtle and we feel the formless Self directly within.

Though it is an impersonal, all-pervasive, unlimited field of Consciousness, the Self works through the symbol to provide the experiences and insights necessary to draw the devotee ever closer. In this way it is possible to have a personal relationship with the Self. Before the devotee is subtle enough to feel God's love, he or she should purify the extroverting *rajasic* and dulling *tamasic* energies through prayer and devotional service

80. The others, discussed above, are: meditation, action and knowledge.

When I love God, in effect I'm loving everyone and everything because God is this whole universe. Clay, for example, might be thought of as the "god" of a pot insofar there is no pot without clay. And just as every atom of the pot is clay, every atom of this world is God, congealed, grossified Love. Until we understand that the whole universe is love we need to see everything as God or a symbol of God – because it is.[81] My spiritual brothers and sisters are true symbols too, "cast in the image of God." And significantly it should not escape my attention that if everyone else is God I too am God and most worthy of worship.[82]

For those uncomfortable seeing humans as symbols of the Divine, any object that invokes love, like a tree, stone, a flower, an animal or religious and mythological symbols is acceptable. However, at some point the meditation needs to include humans insofar as everything eventually needs to be seen as one's own Self – if the path of love is to culminate in Self-realization.[83]

Endow the symbol with noble qualities. The "God" should be compassionate, conscious, all-powerful (capable of fulfilling spiritual and worldly needs), peaceful and beautiful. Installing these qualities in the symbol is a roundabout way of developing them in oneself.

If You Can't Make It, Fake It

Religion or religious concepts need not enter into it. If you have difficulty with the idea of God, adopt any sensible reason for treating everyone with love and respect – because we are all human beings, for example. Or for no reason at all. The path of love simply means loving others for their sake, thinking of them first, helping them. This view is a powerful antidote to the selfish view of love because the devotee is saying, in effect, that the Separation is not real. Eventually, this practice heals the Separation.

Return to the Source

Loved unconditionally, the world starts loving back! The more love is practiced, the more it flows, like a mountain torrent in springtime, flushing away unforgiv-

---

81. It's not actually a symbol, because the universe is non-dual love, but to make the vision of oneness real we need to take everything we see as God until the vision of non-duality happens.

82. This path is an excellent solution to the self-esteem problem.

83. If any object is ultimately excluded, the love that develops will not be unconditional.

ing thoughts and feelings. Slowly attention turns within, awakening the devotee to the unlimited power of Love. When our small loves find their infinite Source we are free and are no longer compelled to grovel at the feet of the world.

Qualifications of a Divine Lover

The path of love, devotion, is an unsentimental discipline of mind, a method of converting emotion into devotion and an effective means of Self-realization. Though it usually begins with some form of religious practice, worship of deities and idols, for example, it culminates in the highest form of realization, union with the Self.

Anyone can practice love, but to achieve Self-realization, the devotee must be ethically and morally pure, endowed with discrimination, dispassion and a burning desire to know God. He or she must be truthful, straightforward, sincere, non-injuring, kind, considerate, polite, compassionate, charitable, forbearing, patient, humble, self-accepting, accommodating, persevering, fearless and mentally strong.

The devotee needs the faith to commit to sustained and persistent effort in restraining the outward flowing tendencies of the heart and directing all feelings toward the Self, a futile practice without an equally strong commitment to the practice of non-attachment.

Non-Attachment

"When the moon shines, the stars dim. When the sun shines, the moon loses luster." ~ an old saying

Such is the self-indulgent nature of the age and the intensity of ego's resistance to the idea of loss that modern writers on spiritual topics have been forced to scotch the words "sacrifice" and "renunciation," and employ the euphemism "non-attachment." Call it what you will, serious devotional progress is impossible without drawing back from outer things and ideas. True renunciation, non-attachment, means that on the physical level the devotee must be willing to abandon craving for the fruits of action; on the intellectual level, self-limiting concepts; and on the emotional level, attachment to love objects.[84]

Contrary to conventional wisdom, renunciation brings power, understanding and love. For example, people willingly sacrifice a less attractive object for

---

84. The attachment, not the object, needs to be renounced.

a more attractive one. When someone addicted to sensuous pleasure discovers the subtler pleasures of the mind, physical objects lose luster. And when the devotee finds the state of Love that is the innermost Self, the small personal loves that captivate the unthinking heart pale. As the practice of letting go grows, love grows.

Peel back the veneer of life and see the love-glue that bonds it to the Self. Strip away the shallow emotions that crave romance and excitement, and discover that your deepest need is the desire to love and be loved. Nothing is more exciting and attractive than love, realizing oneness with someone or something. When the real object of our desire is unknown, we chase small loves, but when we wake up to the Self, we understand that it could only be the Self we love, it is for the sake of the Self that we love. Even our small loves are merely pale reflections of the Love pervading every atom of the universe.

An *Upanishad* says, "None ever loved the husband for the husband's sake; it is the Self, the Lord[85] within, for whom the husband is loved. None ever loved the wife for the wife's sake, but for the sake of the Self in the wife."

The path of love directs love to the Self, the real object of our affections. Passion, feeling and emotion become workable when rightly directed and sublimated into the practice of unconditional love.

The Practice of Love

Although Love is formless and nameless, forms and names can be used to cultivate devotion. Because it produces spiritual *vasanas* and purifies worldliness, physical practice, ritual, which can be discarded at the advanced stages, is the foundation of devotional life. Ritual involves two elements: a devotional attitude and a physical or mental symbol of the Beloved.

Because the mind is gross when we begin, physical images like stone, brass, gold or wooden statuary, a picture or a highly evolved living human are easiest to worship.

The endless smorgasbord of symbols provided by world religions permits the devotee to select one to which he or she is particularly attracted. Religious symbols derive their power by invoking Self archetypes,[86] awakening a sense of awe, majesty, reverence and love.

---

85. The term "Lord" in Vedic literature does not usually refer to a particular deity but the limitless, nameless, formless Self. The term should be taken as someone or something that is valuable, important and powerful.

To still and introvert the mind, the combined power of one's thoughts and feelings need to be directed to the symbol in an attempt to achieve an unbroken flow of devotion.

Because it requires no ritual paraphernalia and can be practiced anywhere, the most simple and effective devotional ritual is wholehearted worship of the Divine Name wherein a particular word (or words) that refers to God is repeated continuously, either aloud or silently, with deep feeling. This practice, like action and knowledge *yoga*, purifies unhealthy *samskaras* and turns the mind inward.

Prayer, congregational worship, study of scripture and the lives of great devotees are equally effective rituals. Try seeing your body and home as God's temple, regarding your spouse and children as God's own, considering every spoken word the name of the Lord and every duty as service of God. Bending, lying or kneeling should be considered prostration to God, walking as circumambulation of the deity, all lights as symbols of the Self, sleep as *samadhi*,[87] rest as meditation and the act of eating as God eating God. In this manner every object and activity loses its secular character and becomes divine through devotional practice.

Love Games

The emotional patterns we bring to life are expressions of *samskaras* from previous births shaped by the immediate childhood environment. When we came in, rarely were we taught that the purpose of life was to love God. Therefore our primary relationships, under the pressure of physical and emotional factors, don't serve spiritual ends. Consequently our adult lives are rife with emotional suffering. Had these fundamental relationships taught us to love ourselves and others unconditionally, a longing for God would never have developed.

The path of love transforms emotional energy into devotion. For example, if a parental relationship functioned successfully, the mind will be naturally loving and respectful. From here it is only a short step to convert the love and respect one feels for elders into love of God. The means of conversion are called "*bhavas*," devotional moods or styles of worship that may lead to Self-realization through love.

---

86. The causal body, the unconscious, is home of the archetypes of release and transcendence as well as the archetypes of suffering. *Yoga* purifies unhealthy *samskaras* and turns the mind inward.

87. A state of complete absorption in the Self.

THE SLAVE

Dasya, the Slave, is based on the idea we are not masters and mistresses of our destinies but slaves to the tyrannical *samskaras*. Who is not chained to physical passions, indentured to selfish feelings, painfully shackled to unforgiving thoughts? The more we strive for freedom, rail against injustice and court empowerment, the more we acknowledge bondage to the unreal.

The Slave is a service-oriented psychology that converts feelings of powerlessness into a positive devotional force. The devotee is enjoined to slavishly worship God and its manifestations, particularly people, with a whole heart. He or she should turn his or her life over to God and become a faithful and diligent executor of God's will. Such devotees need to support and maintain religious, charitable and spiritual institutions, faithfully serve enlightened souls, spiritual teachers and God-intoxicated devotees.

In addition to loyalty and respect, the Slave develops a quiet mind and keen discrimination, qualities necessary to distinguish God's voice from the many self-serving ego voices playing in the mind. Practiced faithfully, this devotional mood reduces ego inflations to rubble as it empowers the inner Self.

THE WIFE

If the Slave is not your cup of tea, try *kanta*, the Wife, another high-devotional stance. The tie between the husband and wife is the strongest and sweetest, containing all expressions of love, particularly sexual intimacy, which symbolizes the union of the devotee and God, the ecstatic wedding of the individual and universal selves. In a mood of complete identification and attachment, the devotee, regardless of sex, sees God as a husband or wife, to honor and obey in every situation, even beyond the grave. Just as devoted spouses gladly suffer for each other, the devotee will suffer any misery for his or her beloved Husband or Wife.

A quotation on the back of an eighteenth-century painting reproduced in a book entitled *Krishna, the Divine Lover* illustrates the mood as practiced by a sect of devotees known as the Shakti Bhavas,[88] worshippers of the Divine Mother, Radha, consort of Krishna: "This sect is in favor with those with an effeminate turn of mind. They declare themselves to be the female companions of Radha, with the idea of paying her homage and establishing identity, even taking on the manner of speech, gait, gestures and dress of women. At monthly intervals, in the manner of menstruating women, they put on red clothes as if affected by menstruation and pass three days in this state. After menstruation is over, they take a ceremonial purificatory bath. In the manner of married women anxious to be physically united with their husbands as enjoined in the scriptures, they take to themselves on the fourth night a painting of Sri Krishna, stretch themselves and raising both legs, utter "ahs" and "oohs," adopt coy womanly manners and cry aloud, "Ah, Krishna, I die! Oh, Krishna, I die!" Through practices like these they believe they earn great merit and please the Lord by engaging themselves the whole night."[89]

THE FRIEND

A more common form of worship, one that transforms worldly love into devotion, is *sakhya*, friendship, in which equal love flows between God and the devotee. God is viewed as a tried and true confidante, a close relative or family member, one with whom innermost secrets can be shared. "Henceforth I call you not servants, for the servant knoweth not what the lord doeth, but I call you friends, for all things I have heard of my Father, I have made known to you." Striving to see everyone in a friendly light, those who practice this devotional mood take great pleasure in encouraging and supporting their friend's spiritual inclinations.

That a competitive ego may develop is thought to be the downside of this type of devotion. The expression popular in New Age circles some years ago, "God is my co-pilot," is a case in point. Nevertheless a diffident, sacrificing attitude toward God, the Friend, is cultivated. As do close friends, the devotee acutely suffers moments of separation, continually craving God's company, either in the form of a deep experience of God or through communion with other devotees. The tender, joyful and playful relationship of nine- and ten-year-old children serves to model this charming mood which sees God as an equal playmate sporting among His or Her creations.

88. *Shakti* is the energetic, feminine aspect of Consciousness. In spiritual literature women tend to symbolize energy and love.

89. Vedic deities invariably have "vehicles" or "*shaktis*," which are usually symbolized by a woman or an animal, the idea being that the non-dual Self can only function through a form or deity. When the Supreme Deity, the Self, is symbolized as a woman, like Kali, the vehicle is invariably an animal, which represents the "lower" nature. So Shiva and Shakti, Ram and Sita, Krishna and Radha represent alternatively the Self and the universe, Spirit and matter, the Self and the mind, although on the rudimentary devotional level they are thought of as actual physical gods and goddesses. This "primitive" conception works because the Self, which dwells in the hearts of all, knows that the prayers are actually for it and compassionately functions through the chosen symbol to fulfill the devotee's needs.

The Child

A popular *bhava*, because we so easily identify with childlike parts of the psyche, this method is based on the universal need of children to love their parents.[90] The devotee is enjoined to love God with the unsuspecting faith of the child, acknowledging and accepting his or her state of total helplessness, ignorance, dependence and attachment. Practically, the devotee is meant to treat all fatherly and motherly figures as God, including his or her own parents. Parents, our physical source, make a nice symbol of God, our spiritual source. The realization that we are part and parcel of His or Her being instills confidence in our own divinity.

Similar to the Slave, this love game is considered an imperfect vehicle for God-realization because it does not, except indirectly, cultivate knowledge of God, leaving the devotee vulnerable to exploitation and manipulation from unconscious forces and religious figures. Ultimately love begets knowledge because the intellect develops curiosity for what the heart loves, but in the short run this devotional stance is at best a preliminary step in the soul's long march home. Because this style of worship produces such deep attachment, unless the devotee cultivates understanding of the formless aspect of God through scriptural study and meditation he or she is in danger of merely using God to satisfy ego needs and will not realize that the need behind needs is union with God. And finally, in this approach the love object is seen as someone other than oneself and therefore rarely leads to Self-realization.

Mom and Pop

Vatsalya, the parental mood, is thought to be superior to the Child because parental love is tempered with understanding and a sense of responsibility. The precious and profound love of God produced by this mood is balanced and enhanced by an equally deep attempt to probe the mysteries of the Divine through scriptural study, meditation and reflection.

Vatsalya taps the parental archetype and can be successfully practiced by anyone who has felt the need to protect and nurture small, helpless creatures. Children, because of their purity, innocence and guileless bliss, make excellent symbols of God. When the devotee develops this feeling for his or her inner Self, he or she shines with maternal or paternal splendor. Because one becomes what one meditates on in time, when maternal feelings for God achieve rap-

90. Perhaps the strident criticism by thinking people of fundamentalism stems from Christianity's obsession with this devotional stance. The idea that "children of God" are meant to obey, not think for themselves, puts them at odds with modern views.

turous intensity this mood is even known to produce mammary secretions in women!

Because it forces the devotee to identify with the "inner parent," this mood helps heal the negative views of parents that accompany the reluctance of adults to leave their "inner child" and attain spiritual maturity. The *bhava* also teaches the devotee to detach from ideas of power, fear and punishment that might be associated with God. Calling into question the concept of mindless obedience, the *bhava* also roots out concepts of devotional unworthiness associated with God's glory, majesty and grandeur – actually projections of a primitive religious consciousness.[91] Unlike children, parents are not generally moved to awe in the presence of the child. Because they cannot beg from the child, the *bhava* negates the tendency to ask favors of the Lord and complain about one's lot. And like parents for their children, the devotee is enjoined to make any sacrifice for the sake of God.

THE PASSIONATE LOVER

....

"Oh, for one kiss from Thy lips,
my Beloved!
The thirst of one kissed by Thee increases forever,
his sorrows vanish and he forgets
all things but Thee."

....

About this kiss, Swami Vivekananda says: "Aspire for that kiss of the Beloved, that touch of the lips that makes the devotee mad, which makes a man a god. To the one who has been blessed with such a kiss, the whole of nature changes, worlds vanish, suns and moons die out, and the universe itself melts away into that one infinite ocean of love. That is the perfection of the madness of love."

A selfless lover eager to gratify his or her beloved is the intriguing model for this *bhava* which takes the bliss of physical orgasm as a symbol of the powerful experience of ecstatic union with the Self.

Sringarasa bhava,[92] the attitude of passionate love of God, is often considered the most advanced love game because passionate spiritual love is the hardest to de-

---

91. In fact God, the Self, is neither great nor small, glorious nor inglorious. And while it seems great and glorious with reference to the ego's smallness and selfishness, to constantly idolize the love object is spiritually unwise, since by implication it diminishes one's own innate greatness. If God is great, I am great. If God is nothing, I am nothing.

velop, owing to the difficulty of consistently experiencing the Self. It is also difficult to break, owing to an excess of attachment brought on by the experience of extreme joy in the presence of God.

A completely spiritual love, the devotee sees God, the innermost Self, as divinely beautiful and lovely, an Adonis or Aphrodite, to be loved with affections verging on the erotic. In this style of love, all conventions, reservations, hesitations and personal views are cast aside and an exclusive, potentially jealous, love cultivated. A gargantuan appetite, craving for the embrace of God, the experience of the Self, is evidenced, the need for spiritual experience replacing the need for physical gratification. Just as lovers locked in the throes of orgasm do not know inside or outside, or which body is which, the devotee in union with the Self sees no distinctions and experiences, only the sweetest bliss.

ABSENCE MAKES THE HEART GROW FONDER

Obstacles to ecstatic meditation – return to mental and emotional states of mind – serve to intensify this *bhava* and are to be used as opportunities to develop love in absence, just as a lover's desire for the beloved is increased by temporal and spatial separation.

It should be noted that this mood in no way resembles the modern idea of *tantra yoga*[93] as "spiritual sex." Based on the fact that true love only comes from within, it is a sophisticated psychological technique for sublimating sexual energy into a high meditative state of mind, and can be successfully practiced only by virtuous, celibate individuals or married souls in mature, non-possessive relationships. Unlike love born of *rajas*,[94] passionate love of God derives from the *sattvic* element and aims to gratify God, the object of one's affections, not the devotee.

The state of mind and the emotions produced by the realization of the presence of God, the deity in the Heart, includes loss of consciousness and suspension of animation as if one were asleep: erratic breathing, perspiration, thrills, chills, horripilations, shivering, breaking voice, change of color and shedding unselfish tears from the sides of the eyes.

92. *Sringarasa* means "springtime" and was chosen to represent this *bhava* because spring is the season of sexual passion.

93. Sexual union is often used as a symbol of the union of the devotee with God, not as a feel-good substitute for Divine Love.

94. *Rajas* invariably inclines one to selfishness.

The devotional manifestations of realization of the absence of God's presence are sleeplessness, helplessness, fickleness, depression and anxiety. When they descend from the ecstatic heights of devotion, devotees practicing this *bhava* often see God as a fickle, inconsiderate and unfaithful lover prone to selfish disappearances. They are not above exhibiting signs of haughty superiority and disdain, fervent yearning, regret because of the Beloved's uncaring attitude and a sense of folly for having become involved with God in the first place. Occasionally the separation causes such anguish the devotee accuses the Lord of cruel injustice and the perverse dispensation of pleasure to others, while the devotee, who has not forgotten the Beloved for a minute, continues to suffer.

FORBIDDEN LOVER

Operating under the assumption that the more love is obstructed the more it intensifies, this mood, a variation of the Passionate Lover, converts feelings of secrecy and shame associated with love into a positive devotional force.

Love of God often awakens in the most unlikely and inconvenient worldly circumstances. When a declaration of love would invite ridicule, condemnation and persecution, taking God as a forbidden lover is helpful. Devoid of outer signs, the Forbidden Lover is a "stealth" psychology through which devotion grows by inner yearning, silent repetition of the Holy Name and meditation. This mood is tailor-made for devotees who need to protect their spirituality from possessive, insecure and jealous spouses.

Negativity

Because it ultimately spells the end of ego control, devotional practice often generates strong ego resistance. Negativity tends to exhaust as devotion develops, but occasionally negative *samskaras* refuse to yield, and require a radical procedure.

Taking a negative attitude toward negativity, thinking of ourselves as worthless sinners, for example, reinforces it, destroys discrimination, clouds self-awareness and derails spiritual practice. Taking a negative attitude toward others is a *karmic* disaster. To deal effectively with negativity, devotional science encourages us to project it at God – as a last resort.

If the purpose of devotional practice is to produce an unbroken flow of thought and feeling in the direction of God, allowing periods of negativity to break the flow is devotionally unwise. Therefore though the offerings are ugly and inappropriate, we should place them squarely on the altar of our deity.

Rather than abandon my practice when I am angry, I need to castigate God for denying me the courage to overcome my weaknesses. Rather than turn my back, why not blame the Lord for turning His or Her back on me? With a little imagination a devotee can dump any kind of negativity at the feet of the Beloved, a practice that protects oneself and the world. When it is given to God, it does not recycle but dissolves like clouds in God's vast inner heaven, filling the heart with love.

As the love offering proceeds, the barrier between the devotee and God becomes increasingly transparent. Repressing negativity solidifies it[95] and erects a thick wall of duality around the ego, cutting it off from the Lord's loving embrace. Ultimately both God and the devotee merge into each other in devotional ecstasy.

How does God, the innermost Self, feel about this practice? Just as a lover listens to the angry tirades of the beloved because the love behind the words is perceptible, God understands the devotee's distress and appreciates his or her desire to maintain contact at all costs, graciously accepting, nay, encouraging, all expressions of love, even foul abuse. Paying attention to God irrespective of the emotional state, the devotee becomes absorbed in God and experiences mystic union.

A touching example of a negative relationship with God is provided by this commentary by H. Poddar on a verse from the *Narada Bhakti Sutras*: "When a child begins to toddle, it often stumbles and falls. Hearing the cry the mother runs to help, but the child becomes angry with the mother for assuming that it might need help, even though she was not at fault, and chides her to make her feel guilty. 'Why did you leave me alone? See what happens when you leave me?' it says. Then it decides to punish her. 'I'll never talk to you,' it wails. 'I'll never sit in your lap!' To appease its anger the mother tries to take it in her arms but it evades her and runs away weeping. Why does it do so? Because it recognizes its power over her and hers over it. She is everything to the child and the child is totally dependent on her. There is no discrimination. The child can express anything without fear, including all its negativity. The dependent devotee makes God the object of passion, anger, and pride."

Peace

This *bhava* is a characteristic of Self-realized souls, devotees with a continuous and direct experience of God. Because spiritual practice as a means of attain-

95. Christ's admonition, "Resist not evil," acknowledges this deep truth.

ment ceases on the realization of the Self, this *bhava* is not actually a practice but a description of the relationship between the mind of a realized soul and the Self. In it the emotions are stilled and fused with the Self, "the peace that passeth understanding." This type of devotee, who is one with God, is a lover of solitude, discriminating and indifferent to his or her own ego. He or she has strong but well-considered opinions, a refined sense of irony and is unaffected by the emotions and views of others.

Development of Devotion

Primary devotion is the state where the devotee and the object of devotion have become one. Secondary devotion is dualistic, a communication between the devotee and an object of devotion, and is conditioned by the instrument of worship, the subtle body. As we have seen, the subtle body is always influenced by the *gunas*, and therefore *sattva*, *rajas* and *tamas* color devotion.

STAGE ONE

When *tamas* predominates, a rudimentary and ignorant style of devotion develops. Because sleepy waves envelop his or her intelligence, the devotee is neither self- nor Self-aware. God, who is known indirectly through blind belief, is worshipped fearfully and slavishly. Such devotees are susceptible to superstitious beliefs in magic, ghosts, evil spirits, poltergeists, demons and devils.

Tamas, the dark energy, dictates a commitment to formula, especially ritual, and literal interpretation of scripture. The unhappy dualistic view of "original sin," which saddles the devotee with a negative identity, is the crest jewel in the *tamasic* devotee's belief system. Ignorance loves organization, swelling the ranks of cults and religious institutions worldwide. Because thinking for oneself is considered a form of disobedience, the *tamasic* devotee is easily manipulated by corrupt priests and is happy to surrender to powerful spiritual personalities. To question or attack this kind of faith is to gain an enemy for life. Religious history is replete with examples of excesses wreaked from this narrow state of mind.

The tendency to worship God or the spiritual teacher as an authoritarian figure is often motivated by the belief in oneself as a helpless child of God. On the positive side, this type of faith is capable of withstanding life's pinpricks and major crises. The conviction that an external God exists is steady, deep and heartfelt.

STAGE TWO

Rajas, the projecting power, keeps the mind and emotions in a continual state of disturbance, which functions as an opaque moving screen, effectively concealing the Self and blocking the flow of love from within. When the *rajasic* devotee's needs are satisfied, the world is a Garden of Eden. When unfulfilled, God often takes the blame.

The *rajasic* devotee's lust for life, ambition and sense of dissatisfaction work against developing a steady stream of love. On the other hand, dissatisfaction can prompt one to enthusiastically purify *tamasic* devotional elements. Because of this, *rajasic* devotion is sometimes considered superior to its *tamasic* sister.

The *rajasic* devotee is inclined to self-centeredness and is not above bargaining with the Lord for power, position and wealth. The theory of "abundance" currently making the rounds on the New Age spiritual circuit is tailor-made for this type of devotee, who tends to be status- and image-conscious, views devotion as evidence of attainment and is not above using it to humiliate and impress others. Scratch the surface and you find a someone more interested in presenting a devotional front to the world than a devotional heart to God. Unlike the steady dependability of the dark type, the active devotee will change religions, beliefs, teachers and practices at the drop of a hat.

Rajasic devotional style, unlike the sleepy innocence of Mother/Father worship, tends to be passionate. In evolved souls God is taken as the ultimate Lover, an appropriate object for intense feelings of romance, attachment, possessiveness, jealousy and anger. For *rajasic* devotion to evolve into *sattva*, the devotee must be convinced that God, not His or Her toys, are the goal of spiritual life. Once committed to the highest view, union with God, the devotee becomes a bundle of spiritual energy and makes rapid progress.

STAGE THREE

With roots in the Absolute, *sattva*, the third strand in the psychic rope and the highest of the three lower stages of devotion, is the most secure foundation for devotional life because the *sattvic* heart is a spotless mirror, capable of accurately reflecting God's image. *Sattvic* devotees are blessed with curiosity, intelligence and discrimination. He or she loves God purely and unselfishly.

Because the veil separating the *sattvic* devotee from God is so thin, the devotee may become spiritually conceited and suffer attachment to goodness, beauty and knowledge, golden chains difficult to break if devotion is to flower into the fourth and highest stage.

Love and Knowledge

As love for God grows, the desire to know more about God increases. And as knowledge of God, based on scripture and direct experience grows, so does love of God. Knowledge of an ego does not incline to love, because egos are selfish and fickle, but knowledge of God invariably increases love because God's nature is eternal love. Therefore both paths, love and knowledge, are intertwined like passionate lovers.

Evolution Through the *Gunas*

Tamas is the devotee's most intractable enemy because its sleepy clouds cover the intellect, veiling the ideal, the state of Supreme Devotion. *Rajas'* unremitting projections also serve to obscure the vision of the goal, but passionate pursuit of spiritual life brings glimpses that inspire continued purification. As striving to experience the Self increases, experience of the Self increases, bringing knowledge of the Self. Knowledge "of" the Self is not Self-knowledge, but may eventually lead to full enlightenment.

In the *sattvic* mind a happy, selfless, blissful state called *rati* arises. The experience of *rati* is so delightful that the devotee becomes quickly attached and purifies more diligently. When *rati* becomes deep and constant it is called *prema*, transcendental Love.

The Goal

....

"Attaining It one becomes intoxicated,
then silent, delighting in the Self."
~ *Narada Bhakti Sutras*

....

The state of devotion to which this verse refers is not a simple love of God inspired by blind belief, but an inner transformation, the rebirth of the soul out of the womb of matter into the realm of pure Spirit. It is a spontaneous awakening to the ultimate state of Being, an ecstatic, expansive, dynamic, open-ended experience that fills the head with wisdom and the heart with love. Unlike "born again" experiences, which quickly fade, leaving the devotee caught up in the limitations of the old life, the heart merges completely and permanently into the Self.

Even a glimpse of this state inspires intense faith, prompting a single-minded striving to enter into It. Referred to as salvation in religion, and liberation or enlightenment in the spiritual world, it is beyond meditative, concentrated, absorbed and practice-induced states of mind.

This seeing and enjoying the Self inspires divine madness. The devotee feels exhilarated and intoxicated, as if he or she had won the lottery and fallen in love on the same day. It is not unlike a mother's feeling, extended forever, when a child thought to be dead returns to her. When it happens the devotee is blown away and no sense of separateness remains. Everyone and everything is experienced as pure undying love. One may hug and kiss a complete stranger, sweetly accept an insult, go without eating for days, renounce money and possessions, sing recklessly, laugh without reason like a child or talk wildly in tongues.

Gradually, however, the emotions purify. Not that the vision of God is less intense or the relationship less passionate, but the heart breaks open and becomes infinitely spacious, graciously accommodating the Divinity blazing within. Over time the feelings, in an orgy of sacrifice, offer themselves to the fire, like a moth to a flame – and visible signs of devotion disappear. God doesn't seem like such an incredible being anymore, but a trusted companion.

The devotee will shortly become aware of a deafening silence, a powerful presence that swallows every thought and feeling, engulfing every perception. Caught in the embrace of timeless love, mad passion becomes the white heat of meditation and the devotee sits quietly sipping the nectar flowing from the Heart of hearts. Becoming silent, absorbed in the Infinite, the patterns supporting the ego crumble, the mind disappears like a phantom, and the soul in primordial nakedness realizes oneness with the Self.

CHAPTER V
Fine Points

THE DIVISION OF the modern psychological world into physical, emotional and cognitive therapies suggests parallels to the paths of action, devotion and knowledge outlined in the two preceding chapters. Dominated almost exclusively by Freud's ideas for most of the twentieth century, the therapeutic world might be seen as a secular attempt to compete with religion in the business of cleaning up sinners. Its model of the ego, which sees childhood trauma and libidinal impulses as the cause of suffering, was taken as seriously as church doctrine by a significant segment of the thinking public for the better part of the century. Because it takes the ego as the only self, it has suffered since its inception from the absence of an overarching concept like the Self to integrate its diverse psychologies. And because it is saddled with the materialist-scientific model of the universe, it has until recently steadfastly denied the validity of spiritual experience.

The correction began almost immediately with the schism between Freud and Jung. Unlike Freud, Jung couldn't deny spiritual experience and developed the idea of the collective unconscious, a quirky Western blend of the causal body and the Self. Jung's work set the stage for the transpersonal model that sprang up as a result of the influx of Vedic and Buddhist ideas in the sixties and seventies.

The increasingly popular transpersonal model, which has established itself as a legitimate branch of therapy in the last thirty years, is closer to the original spirit of the *Vedas* in that it acknowledges one of the most sought-after experiences – transcendence – and is therefore not antagonistic to meditation and spiritual experience.[96]

Transcendence is not world-denying or ego-destroying, but inclusive of both ego and world. Fundamentally, it is simply a shift from a particular to a

---

96. Because Jung did not realize the Self in its state beyond the macrocosmic causal body (which he called the collective unconscious), he located it as an "archetype," or *samskara*, in the causal body. He was unable to see that the Self transcended the causal body, because his official means of knowledge was inferential – the interpretation of dreams. His direct personal experience of the Self, even had he been able to contextualize and interpret it correctly, would never have been accepted by the scientific community, so it was professionally useless. He was incapable of understanding the full import of his Self research because it occurred in a spiritual vacuum, the Western scientific intellectual world. Had he been brought up in

universal view of oneself and one's world. The transpersonal model, which is a reasonable compromise between enlightenment as a blissful daily experience and the myopic life of a neurotic, materialistic ego, is a rudimentary purification therapy insofar as it addresses the larger issues of values and purpose. When we consciously know that lasting happiness is the purpose of life, we make a giant step spiritually because we free ourselves of the frustrating view that activities, experiences and objects will relieve our sense of limitation.

When values are sorted out, most of our suffering dissolves. Values, which scientific-materialist therapies are loath to tackle and which religion approaches in an unhelpful moralistic way, are related to ego in that the more limited one's conception of oneself, the more selfish one's values. The more selfish one's values, the more one finds oneself in conflict with oneself and others.

The three-*guna* model presented in Chapter III explained the unconscious forces operating in every personality – *sattva* (light), *rajas* (passion) and *tamas* (inertia) – and suggested that the ego/mind of a psychologically mature person was predominantly *sattvic*. The unhealthy or "dysfunctional" complexes that need purifying before the individual can live an integrated life were said to be caused by excessive *tamas* and *rajas* in relation to *sattva*. When one's natural spiritual light, or consciousness, is veiled by heavy *tamasic* clouds, the ego/mind is dominated by fear and aversion. *Rajas*, like *tamas*, is a deep unconscious reaction to the separation of the ego from the Self, and produces a passionate, aggressive, tension-filled mind. When the relative proportions of *rajas* and *tamas* are reduced and accommodated within a spacious *sattvic* mind, they cease to produce negative emotions and become forces for growth and change. *Rajas* provides the motivational energy for realizing goals, and *tamas* the grounding required to protect and maintain what has been achieved, spiritual or otherwise. A mind dominated by *rajas* and *tamas* is a suffering mind. When *rajas* and *tamas* are the sole energies operating, serious psychological dysfunction, like manic depression [bipolar disorder], can occur. Mania is total *rajas* and depression is complete *tamas*. To use modern psychological language, the more fear and desire operate in the personality, the less integrated and more dysfunctional it is. In terms of Vedic science, such a personality is said to be "impure," the standard being the pure[97] Self.

Vedic culture where both the unconscious and the Self have been accepted knowledge for at least three thousand years and figure prominently in both Yoga and Vedanta, his research would undoubtedly have met with considerable support and led him quickly to a clear understanding of the relationship between the Self and the causal body.

The Unhealthy Mind

Rather than connecting all the modern words describing psychological dysfunction with *rajas* and *tamas*, suffice it to say that a psyche in which guilt (*tamas*), fear (*tamas*), denial (*tamas*), projection (*rajas*), anger (*rajas*), passion (*rajas*), aggression (*rajas*), defensiveness (*tamas*), desire (*rajas*), greed (*rajas*), stress (*rajas*), depression (*tamas*) and fantasy (*rajas*) operate is impure. Since everyone exhibits these unhealthy psychological tendencies to some degree, we all have work to do.

The popularity of transcendence as a solution to suffering might be reasonably tied to the degree of unfinished inner work. The more one suffers, the stronger the desire for freedom. Conversely the more integrated the personality, the less the desire for change. So in this age of instant gratification, the tedium of *sadhana* is readily sacrificed for the transcendental quick fix. However, transcendence as an escape from suffering is difficult to "maintain" without *sadhana* because powerful *samskaras* activate the ego and pull the mind back down to the *karmic* level.

The Integrated Person

To get to the point where meditation provides easy access to the Self and a healthy ego becomes just another of the many objects in one's consciousness, the ego needs *sadhana*. However, ultimately *sadhana* is only a means to an end. When it ceases to be a discipline and becomes a natural way of life, the meditator is psychologically healthy and qualified to enter the final stage of life – Self-inquiry – which will solve the riddle of identity.

Qualifications

What is a healthy, qualified mind?

(1) An open mind, one willing to see itself differently. Because of the subtle nature of meditation and the difficulty in objectively evaluating experience, the meditator should seek the help of scripture and the counsel of realized souls. The mind that imagines that it is qualified to interpret its own experience, spiritual or otherwise, solely on the basis of its beliefs and opinions is not ready to assume the impersonal view propounded by the spiritual science, and is therefore unqualified for meditation. Although the impersonal view is not Self-realization, it is a necessary stage because it purifies the effects of non-apprehension of the Self, i.e. limited conceptions and the disturbing emotions

---

97. Pure means "partless." The Self is a partless whole.

they produce. Eventually even the idea "I am limitless awareness" dissolves into the permanent knowing experience of oneself as the Self. The mind that expects a grand enlightenment experience to cancel its ignorance, and therefore refuses to examine its beliefs and opinions, is not qualified for enlightenment.

The Importance of a Teacher

It is remarkable that people who would not think twice about investing years studying with top professionals in their chosen fields will shun spiritual teachers and attempt meditation based on the instructions contained in a ten-dollar New Age cassette. In an age of instant gratification, sound bites and fast food, it is not surprising that we have come to believe that a few minutes of deep breathing, concentrating on the space between the eyebrows, parroting a *mantra* or sashaying through a visualization fantasy will produce transcendence.

On the other hand, because spirituality is totally unregulated, setting standards by which techniques, teachings and teachers can be objectively evaluated, is impossible. So the situation is potentially dangerous – a further reason why a mature mind is required. Nonetheless, a respectable teacher, purified of the craving for pleasure, power, fame and wealth, will appear when the subtle body is clean and the desire for liberation intense.

Meditators need help developing an objective view because the ego has a vested interest in keeping its dark penumbra cast over the mind. Secondly, since the Self is so subtle and the techniques for reaching it equally subtle and varied, the assistance of someone who has successfully walked the path is invaluable.

However, a meditator should view all teachers, *gurus,* meditation masters and their teachings unsentimentally. Suspending critical faculties and dredging a wide moat of superstitious love and respect between the meditator and the teacher, though passing for devotion in certain circles, is certain to nullify the benefits conferred by association with a realized soul.

The open mind is a thoughtful mind, one endowed with a clear understanding of its own psychology and the theory and practice of meditation. Binge meditators, who vacillate between intense practice and worldly life, don't understand the fundamental ideas behind the spiritual path. A thoughtful mind, one that takes the long-range and objective view, refuses to cease discriminating when powerful experiences are taking place.

(2) A discriminating mind, one convinced that the Self alone is real and that the phenomenal worlds, subtle and gross, the not-Self,[98] are unreal.

What is reality? Reality, the Self, exists in the past, present and future, before the past and after the future, and in and beyond the waking, dream and deep sleep states of consciousness. Any object, event or state of mind that doesn't satisfy this definition is considered unreal or "not-Self."

On an outer level, discrimination is the power to avoid entanglements in the dramas, pleasures and concerns of daily life. To the discriminating, life is viewed as a fantasy, a tragicomedy to be acted to the hilt, no doubt, but ultimately of no lasting consequence. On the inner level, discrimination forces the meditator to take his or her likes and dislikes, memories, dreams, fears, desires, "altered" or "spiritual" states of mind as transitory epiphenomena. Both outer and inner phenomena are to be considered not-Self, or unreal.[99]

"Unreal" does not mean objects do not experientially exist but that their existence depends on many temporal factors. Reality, the Self, is self-existent, and therefore independent of all phenomena. A rainbow, for example, momentarily exists but is not real, because it relies on a conspiracy between a specific sense organ and certain physical conditions. When the conditions that brought it into being dissolve, it ceases to exist.

(3) A dispassionate mind is free of the pernicious effects of binding *vasanas*. Dispassion is defined as the willingness to abandon sense-indulgence, emotional passion and intellectual pleasure for the sake of a quiet mind. The meditator should sin intelligently, walking the tightrope between indulgence and abstinence.[100] When indulgence causes attachment, train the mind to let go of the attachment. When denial causes cravings that can't be renounced, indulge in the object until the developing attachment significantly disturbs the mind. Both unfettered indulgence and fanatical denial produce turbulence and prevent meditation. A dispassionate mind, one free of *rajas* and *tamas*, enjoys an ironic, humorous indifference toward itself and the world.

(4) A quiet, balanced mind. The quiet mind will not happen until the first four qualifications develop. The ability to control reactions[101] to stimuli pouring into the mind[102] and repeatedly return one's attention to the Silence creates a steady mind. If subjective baggage – emotional problems, for example – is taken to be real, the mind will never become calm. A calm

---

98. See the chart in Chapter II.

99. The determination of the unreality of phenomena is meant to neutralize the meditator's projections. When the projections are removed and the Self realized, phenomena are once again seen as real because they are known to be non-different from the Self.

100. The Buddha called this *madyamika*, "the middle way."

mind will concentrate on subtle objects, contemplate the inner meaning of the teachings, listen to the Silence and discriminate between the Self and its numerous shadows.

Equanimity is the peaceful state ensuing when the mind meditates consistently on the Silence and detaches itself over and over from sense stimuli, feeling and thought as a result of a continuous examination of their defects.[103]

(5) A motivated mind. Only a burning desire for liberation will generate the perseverance and determination required to overcome the surfeit of obstacles encountered on the path. However, half-hearted motivations may bear fruit if the meditator associates with realized souls and practices renunciation and meditation.

(6) A forbearing mind, one endowed with the capacity to endure sufferings and disappointments without struggling for redress or revenge. An ego that tries to right wrongs or one that feels deprived or victimized is not qualified for meditation.

(7) A believing mind, one capable of taking on faith, pending confirmation through experience, the idea of enlightenment and the words of scripture and realized souls.

(8) A devoted mind. Perhaps the most important qualification, devotion is the constant inquiry into the Self and the determined attempt to incorporate the insights gained through *sadhana* and meditation into one's life.

When the qualities are in full flower, the meditator is spiritually mature and capable of scaling the sacred heights of Self-realization.[104]

---

101. Stimuli, both internal and external, are uncontrollable. Whether or not one reacts and how one reacts, however, can be brought under conscious control. The lion's share of *vipassana* practice, for example, involves controlling reactions by naming and observing sensations in the body and mind. Naming objectifies phenomena and breaks the subjective connection with them.

102. Mental disturbance arises automatically when sensory input interacts with the *vasanas* gurgling up from the causal body. *Samskaras* cannot be controlled by the mind, but need to be sublimated into spiritual practices.

103. Their defect, impermanence, makes them unsuitable as objects of meditation and the basis of life choices.

104. For more on this topic, see "Qualifications of a Divine Lover" in Chapter IV.

How Pure Is Pure?

The purification brought about by *sadhana* is the result of a consistent and continued performance of certain gross and subtle actions over time. As the mind purifies, the meditator increasingly experiences happiness and is tempted to conclude that intensifying *sadhana* will produce lasting happiness. But as personal *samskaras* exhaust and become less binding, another problem develops. The subconscious, the container for personal *samskaras,* is a subset of the collective unconscious, the macrocosmic causal body, the container of the collective *vasanas.* These *vasanas,*[105] which are operating in the background at the beginning stages of spiritual practice, gradually come to the fore as personal complexes yield to the consistent pressure of *sadhana.* Because on a deeper level we are all part of the macrocosmic mind, society's impurities are to some degree our own. Purifying the *vasanas* of every sentient being is so obviously impossible that **eventually the meditator needs to draw the line on the purification idea and seriously face the "who am I?" question.** Because I, the Self, am already pure, I will not practice meditation and *sadhana* for the purpose of purification. Nor will I try to fix the world – which is fine as it is. Moreover, on the ego level, the suffering we are so eager to remove is spiritually valuable insofar as it compels us to look at our values and the way we approach life.

How does purification relate to Self-realization?

Enlightenment takes place in the subtle body. The Self is already enlightened. Enlightenment is the steadfast and simple knowledge "I am whole and complete, limitless awareness." This knowledge, which is based on direct experience of the Self, destroys the ignorance "I am incomplete, inadequate and limited." Obviously, the subtle body of a heroin addict, whose *samskaras* are so powerful that craving dominates the mind from dawn until dusk and in whom even common-sense knowledge does not find a hospitable environment, will be unable to grasp the fact that "I am whole and complete, actionless awareness." On the other hand, a discriminating and dispassionate mind, occasionally rocked by turbulence, can retain this subtle fact. Therefore for practical purposes **we can say that the mind is pure when it is capable of permanently grasping this knowledge.**

When the mind is pure, spiritual experience is prone to occur, but evaluating experience without Self-knowledge is a problem. For example, the Self can be experienced as radiant light, infinite sound, deep peace, power, transcendence, wholeness, a deity, "guidance" and in numerous other ways. If it is

---

105. Political, social, humanitarian and economic "issues" that one feels the need to address.

experienced as deep peace at one sitting, a circumferenceless light at another and the word of God at a third, contradictory understandings about its nature are likely to develop. The argument that one "knows" in an intuitive or mystical way is not helpful, because what happens when "intuition" is not functioning? Self-knowledge, enlightenment, needs to be working in the mind all the time, not only in certain states. Otherwise, how will it free one from the incessant push and pull of the *samskaras*, not to mention the fundamental problem – the concept of oneself as an experiencer conditioned by experience?

Experience and Knowledge Again

If I cannot see the thread running through every daily experience, how am I going to see the thread running through all my diverse inner experiences? In fact the thread running through each inner and outer experience is the experiencer, me, the Self. By knowing my nature I provide myself with the information necessary to make sense of all the contradictions experience has to offer. Receiving teaching at the feet of a realized soul and knowledge of the import of scripture combined with meditation *sadhana* is the traditional means of experiencing and knowing the Self and evaluating experience-based knowledge.

Self-knowledge takes place when the meditator's intellect integrates two apparently different realities, the Self and the not-Self. The "intellect" that makes the discrimination between the Self and the not-Self is a *sattvic* subtle body in which the mind, intellect and ego are integrated and turned inward – not our everyday unpurified mind. This is why enlightenment usually only comes after considerable purification of the *rajasic* and *tamasic samskaras*, either through spiritual practice or prolonged experience of the Self[106] – and why many enlightenments are consequently premature. A period of clarity might allow the meditator to realize the Self, but unexhausted *samskaras* can boil up and disturb the mind to such a degree that the knowledge is lost. However, additional purification brings the knowledge back.

Very often Self-knowledge comes by default as a result of conducting a proper analysis of the mind and ego. It is the knowledge "I am not the ego/mind" that destroys the meditator's identification and attachment to these limited and unreal factors, not a particular mystic experience, although it may

---

106. This is not argument against "experience of" the Self. However, unless inquiry continues during Self-experience, how will the knowledge "I am the Self" occur, since the Self will be taken as just another object of experience? In reality, the Self can't be the object of experience, because it is the ultimate subject and illumines both the relative subject, the ego, and its objects of experience.

come during such an experience. One never "attains" enlightenment, because it's our birthright. One simply removes the identification with the ego/mind.

The view that enlightenment is knowing who one is contradicts the ill-considered view that the intellect needs to be transcended or destroyed for enlightenment to happen, an idea that is probably partly the result of a perennial misinterpretation of the second of Patanjali's *Yoga Sutras*: "yoga chitta vritti nirodha." The verse, which is the basis of the idea of *vasana* purification explained in Chapter II, says that the union[107] (*yoga*) of the individual and the Self is not accomplished until the *samskaras (chitta vrittis)* are exhausted (*nirodha*). If the intellect itself is defined as a *chitta vritti*, which it is from the Self's point of view, then *yoga* takes place. *Yoga* means "union" with the Self.[108] *Yoga*, which in its highest sense is *nirvikalpa samadhi*, the blank or empty mind, is often held up as tantamount to enlightenment. However, if the ego/intellect is responsible for ignorance, how will the *samadhi* remove it if it is not there in the *samadhi*?[109] Even the claim that *nirvikalpa samadhi* is the experience of limitless bliss has to be incorrect, because it presupposes an experiencer and an object of experience, both dualistic thoughts (*chitta vrittis*). If there is no one "there" in that meditation, who is to experience or know what? The case for *yoga* as liberation is more reasonable if we consider *savikalpa samadhi*, which is *samadhi* "with thought." In this case, if we interpret "with thought" as a *sattvic* intellect,

107. Whether this "union" is a matter of experience, knowledge or realization (knowledge/experience) is for the meditator to determine. I am in favor of the knowledge idea, not because spiritual experience is illegitimate, but because of the mind's tendency to cling to the belief that its sense of limitlessness is only available when a certain kind of experience is happening, i.e. when the mind is empty and/or happy. In fact the Self is limitless irrespective of ego's experiencing. And if I have discovered that I am the Self, I do not forfeit limitlessness when the subtle body is suffering or enjoying. I may even find its states amusing.

108. Vedanta argues that there is no one other than the Self to join with it. But Vedanta is forced to admit the existence of an equivalent someone who is ignorant of the Self, so its teachings can remove the ignorance. Even if the one who is ignorant of the Self is the Self, which is impossible, it still has to admit the existence of ignorance – which is equally not-Self.

109. This discussion is not meant to criticize Yoga in favor of Vedanta. In fact the most influential figure in the Vedantic world, the eighth-century non-dualist Shankaracharya, uses the Yoga language of *samadhi* alongside the Vedantic language of *jnanam*, knowledge. (See *Vivekachoodamani* [*The Crest Jewel of Discrimination*] and other texts.) My view is that the *yogis* who attain liberation make the discrimination the Vedantins say is necessary for liberation in *savikalpa samadhi*.

one relatively free of *rajas* and *tamas*, the projecting and veiling energies, we have a situation tantamount to the one above where an awake, alert, inquiring mind is present in meditation to remove its ignorance.

In *savikalpa samadhi* the meditator is seeing from the Self, hence the term *samadhi*, which means that everything seen is equal in value to everything else. The mind is active, hence the word *vikalpa* (thought, feeling, perception), but no thought is more important than any other. Everything is equal because it is known to be the non-dual Self. Seeing things equally destroys the belief that everything is unique and needs to be related to dualistically.

Stuck in Sattva

The blissful state that happens when the subtle body is predominately *sattvic* is often taken as an experience of the Self. The mind becomes increasingly *sattvic* as *rajas* and *tamas* purify. The *gunas* operate sequentially in an unbroken circle. *Tamas* may predominate momentarily with *sattva* and *rajas* dormant, but when *rajas* takes over the mind becomes active. Breaks in the projecting energy indicate that either *tamas* or *sattva* is about to reassert itself. If the meditator notices tiredness while the mind is active, *tamas* is waiting in the wings, opting to become the dominant energy. But if a flash of happiness or peace is experienced, *sattva* is about to take over. By meditating on this shiver of happiness, the *sattvic guna* can be expanded because it increases the happiness *vasana*. If the relative proportions of *rajas* and *tamas* are reduced by practice of the *yogas* as enjoined in Chapter III, the mind experiences many happy periods throughout the day – what might be called intermittent happiness. When the *sattvic* element is more powerful, and the *rajasic* and *tamasic* elements largely effaced through *sadhana* and meditation on these positive feelings, happiness becomes oceanic and breaks like waves over and over again on the shore of the lake of the mind. Eventually, if *sattva* completely dominates the other *gunas*, it will produce light, levitation-like feelings that pervade every atom of the body and cause sustained sensations of ecstasy in the mind.

Joy Is the Enemy

The predominance of *sattva* is both unhelpful and helpful. It is unhelpful because intense and sustained bliss produces reactions of excitement and clinging, which point to remnants of unpurified *rajas* and *tamas*. Unfortunately, a pure mind is still an insentient object, a product of *karma* and needs to be dismissed as "not-Self." It is also unhelpful unless the meditator is extremely dispassionate and clear about the goal, because he or she can become convinced that a pure mind is enlightenment,[110] stop inquiring and terminate the *sadhana*. But because a pure mind is produced by conscious or unconscious *sadhana, rajasic* and *tamasic* "defilements" will eventually reappear unless *sadhana* is continued. After learning the secret of *sadhana*, many settle for *sattvic*-mind happiness and remain in "the world"[111] to act out residual *vasanas* – often burdened with predictably elitist views.

The feeling of satisfaction associated with a pure mind can easily sidetrack inquiry. Absorption in *sattva* is usually proportional to the memory of suffering in *rajasic* and *tamasic* states. The *sattvic* subtle body is blissful because it accurately mirrors the Self. Since the Self is whole and limitless, it translates into a feeling of happiness in the mind. But the experience of wholeness, happiness or bliss characterizing the *sattvic* mind is not liberation, lasting Happiness, because *rajasic* and *tamasic* tendencies can destroy it.

Yet *sattva* is also desirable because a reflective mind is ideal for insight. Moreover, a blissful mind aids concentration. Concentration is necessary for successful meditation on the Silence. The danger, as usual, is ego's tendency to opt for experience in favor of knowledge and attempt to expand the feelings of happiness to infinity. The need to experience infinite happiness is evidence of an unenlightened ego.

Happiness is not the Self, but Self-knowledge causes happiness. It is not the Self because it is insentient and an object of the Self's consciousness. Happiness doesn't know you, but you know happiness. **The realization that one is separate from happiness is one of the final moments in the spiritual quest because it allows the attention to become completely steady and dispassionate.**

Equanimity: Meditation on the Silence

The meditator enters this final stage of meditation when the attention is withdrawn from the experience of happiness and moved to the "space" surrounding it, the Silence. Space is a common Self symbol and need not be taken literally. Meditation on material space is virtually impossible and would not produce the knowledge needed to remove the ignorance of who one is. The Self is often referred to as "space" because it is relatively non-material with reference to the four gross elements; it pervades the elements though none pervade it and it contains the four elements, just as the Self contains all five.

110. This view is popular in both Buddhism and Yoga.

111. There is no world apart from the mind.

Moving the attention from the blissful *sattvic* mind to the silent "space" surrounding it is meditation, direct absorption in the Silence. The attention that meditates on the Silence will become completely balanced. An equanimous mind is capable of discriminating between itself and the Self. Or, if you prefer the language of experience, the equanimous mind "dissolves into" or "becomes" the Self.

Negating the not-Self does not condemn the meditator to a monastic, objectless life. Its purpose is to destroy the belief that happiness is in objects by showing the mind the pure Self. Though the Self is always pure, until enlightenment it is always confused with objects, particularly subtle states of mind. Once the objects have been negated and the Self realized, the objects are re-embraced and life goes on quite normally, the only difference (and what a difference!) being that they produce no attractive or aversive reactions. Or if they do, the reactions are witnessed as not-Self.

The Problem of Language

Because knowledge comes in the form of ideas, and ideas come in the form of language, the language we use to identify the Self may affect our inquiry – since we need knowledge to inquire. The *Vishuddi Magga*,[112] an ancient Pali text which talks about the progressive stages of meditation, shows how language can skew understanding. The text says, "Then, turning away from the contemplation of space, the meditator proceeds to the contemplation of the state of consciousness itself which has arisen with space as its base." The author of a book[113] discussing this state of meditation calls this "becoming aware of awareness." The text continues, "And once the meditator has become aware of awareness" – which is an experience – "he or she should proceed to repeatedly name it, saying, 'Consciousness, consciousness.'"

Naming objectifies and identifies. And if the purpose of meditation is knowledge of the Self, the meditator needs to identify Consciousness. So both languages operate here: the meditative experience, the "contemplation of the state of consciousness which has arisen with space as its base," and the knowledge of it. If the ultimate purpose of the path of meditation were only experience, no need to name the experiences would arise. But at each increasingly

112. *The Path of Purification.*

113. *Tranquility and Insight* by Amadeo Solé-Leris.

subtle stage of meditation the meditator is asked to identity the object of meditation with a word that effectively identifies it as "not-Self."

Because it becomes confusing at this point, let us take issue with the idea of meditating on subtle states of mind and its language of experience, and shift to discrimination and the language of knowledge. For example, the text says, "The meditator proceeds [from the contemplation of happiness] to the contemplation of the state of consciousness itself, which has arisen with space as its base." Oddly, the statement seems to suggest that consciousness arises from matter, which is precisely the epiphenomenal view of modern science and is contrary to all known sources of spiritual wisdom. But the verse says "state" of consciousness. A state must necessarily be distinct from non-dual Consciousness, the Self, which has no states. So this "state" is a condition created when one meditates on Consciousness, i.e. it is a particular experience, "becoming aware of awareness," to use experiential language.

Let us stick with the language of knowledge because the language of experience leaves us in the dark about the most important factor, the meditator. Who or what is the meditator? We have three factors: an object of meditation (awareness, or consciousness), a meditator and the "state" that arises as a result of the contact of the subject with the object. The discrimination between the Self and the not-Self, the subject and objects, asks us to find out who the meditator is. Is the meditator conscious or unconscious? Is the consciousness that "has arisen with space as its base" the same or different from the consciousness of the meditator? The language of experience would seem to suggest that it's different. **The odd paradox of the craving for experience is the blindness of the experiencer to his or her Self.** In fact we never experience objects "out there" in a world apart. So-called "objective" experience is simply experience of oneself apparently conditioned by objects. This is why the purpose of meditation is Self-knowledge, not the experience of a particular state or purification of the mind, since knowledge removes the mistaken belief that experience of something other than oneself is the source of happiness.

The language of identity and knowledge categorically states that the subject and the object are one. Moreover, the purpose of meditation is to discover this fact by "merging" in knowledge the meditator and the object of meditation, freeing the ever-free subject from its love affair with objects. The merger can only happen in knowledge because the subject and object are already one in reality. That they seem separate is caused by the unconscious assumption that the way we perceive things is correct.

In the case of the meditation we're discussing, the "consciousness based on space" is not the Self but an experience in the subtle body of the meditator. Because it is unchanging and all-pervasive, Consciousness can't move to another location. So any movement is simply the apparent movement of thought as it arises and subsides in awareness.

The Nature of the Self

As I sit, my attention completely balanced and riveted on the Silence, I need to stay thoughtful and alert, not fall into a delicious, mindless ecstasy, because I know that the ultimate purpose of meditation is knowledge. At this point knowledge of the Self and the not-Self should be systematically working in my mind so I can very clearly distinguish the meditator-me from me, the object of meditation. **That there is ultimately no distinction should not prevent me from going through the process over and over, until I directly understand how the unchanging Self apparently becomes the ever-changing not-Self, and every last shred of doubt that we are separate is removed.**

Words: Valuable Knowledge

A small child, offered the choice between a candy bar and a one-hundred-dollar bill, will invariably choose the candy. If it is going to destroy my incorrect self-idea, the knowledge operating in my mind when I am meditating needs to help me recognize the truly valuable Self and dismiss the apparently valuable not-Self. So to avoid the problem of language we encountered in the example above, let us unfold the meaning of a few words to facilitate our inquiry.

Three pairs of ordinary words convey important knowledge about who I am and who I am not: **changing** and **changeless**; permanent and impermanent; ephemeral and eternal.

What changes is not me. What does not change is me. What in my meditation is changing? If I am body-conscious, I notice sensations appearing and disappearing in the body. The rising and falling of thoughts and feelings, memories, perceptions, imaginations and visions in the Silence indicate an active mind. Where there are no thoughts and feelings, as in deep sleep and the Self, the mind is inactive. Since mental-emotional phenomena change continually, they are not me either. As obvious as this seems, I need to seriously contemplate this fact because when I descend from my meditative heights, knowledge should be at my fingertips to keep me out of trouble. If a sexual desire is dismissed as laughably unreal in the seat of meditation, is it considered equally unreal when a luscious and inviting body shows up in real life asking for you-know-what. What changes is unreal. What doesn't is real.

Now we have four words to work with: change, changeless, **real** and **un-real**. Let us add two more: **dual** and **non-dual**. The duality I experience in everyday life shows up in meditation as me, the subject, and the objects of my experience. The objects are not real. The subject is real. In real life the objects are gross and subtle, and in meditation, assuming I have transcended body-consciousness, the objects are subtle (*sattvic, rajasic* and *tamasic* states of mind) and very subtle: the Silence. If I am experiencing the Silence, it is an object, and I am the subject. Discerning the nature of the Silence is difficult because it is the subtlest manifestation of the Self, assuming it is not simply the absence of physical noise. If it is the absence of thought, it is the Self.

Which brings us to two more words: **thinkable** and **unthinkable**. Any changing object is thinkable, known by the mind – but am I thinkable? So as I sit with my mind steady on the Silence, unaffected by random thoughts, I might profitably try to see if I can think me. If I can I've got the unreal me, the ego, and need to keep working. **When one inquires into the ego, tries to see what's there, one can't find anything.** The words that help us here are "thing" and "nothing." A "thing" is thinkable, an object of one's consciousness. "Nothing" is not thinkable. I am no "thing," the absence of things. Words fail at this point because it is obvious that I am something if I am alert, present and inquiring into reality. So I need to see how the something that I am is not an object of anyone or anything. Put succinctly, I need to see that I am the thinker, the one wielding the intellect. In ordinary states of mind neither the intellect nor the Self could be said to be the thinker, because our thought life is simply a completely unconscious outpicturing of the *vasanas* – thought thinking itself.

The realization that one is no thing should bring a sigh of relief, but is often cause for lament. Much ado has been made of this fact and it is perhaps the primary reason enlightenment is often assumed to be a negative state. *Nirvana*, for instance, is a legitimate negative statement about the nature of the Self. The Self is not a thing or a state called *nirvana*, but *nirvana* is a word indicating that the Self is thingless, that experience – which relies on objects – is non-existent or "blown out." The word *nirvana* means "blown out." Inquiry into it does not reveal a wanting entity or any objects of experience. When we come to voidness (the no-thingness) we need to continue our inquiry, not stop because we have drawn the conclusion that the Self is a life-denying, scary state. We need to see that what we are seeing is no thing. Yet this no-thing is obviously known by something. And that something is me, the meditator, the Self.

Other pairs of useful words that open up our meditation on the Self and the not-Self are **seer** and **seen**; perceiver and perceived; knower and known; observer and observed; witness and witnessed. The inner world provides many interesting experiences. For example, I may experience limitless light. Sometimes I hear infinite sound. During another session I have profound visions. What do these experiences mean? The discriminating meditator dismisses them all because they are perceived, seen and known – and because they are unreal. Why are they unreal? Because they are limited. They come and go as I watch. And they are not there when I am no longer in meditation. Yet one factor consistently transcends every inner (and outer) experience: me, the observer, the seer.

If everything is the Self and the Self is non-dual, and I am the Self, there can by definition be no witness – since a witness implies the witnessed. This is why it is said that before enlightenment can happen, one needs to remove the witness. The removal of the witness is not a volitional act, physically removing something, but the removal in one's understanding of the belief that the witness and the witnessed are separate objects. Enlightened beings experience objects distinct from themselves just like the rest of us, but they know that duality is a trick of the mind, not an actual fact. For example, a father and his son experience a mirage. The son rushes off to drink, yet the equally thirsty father stays put because he knows that his mind is simply producing the appearance of water.

The most common meditation experience is transcendence, seeing the mind and body as objects, an experience that in itself has no power to liberate – although it might be emotionally liberating. In fact many who experience transcendence come away confused and frightened because they believe that the separation of the Self from the not-Self is unnatural – a confusion caused by ignorance. If, however, a meditator courts transcendence and experiences it armed with the understanding that the seer is the Self and the seen, and the objects are not-Self, or unreal, enlightenment can happen. This knowledge is extremely useful, the means of liberation, even though it takes place in the intellect.[114] But it is not "intellectual," because it is more than the belief of someone who has not experienced the separation of the Self from its vehicles first-hand.

What is my nature? **Consciousness.** Before we use this idea in meditation we need to know that the normal definition of consciousness is spiritually incorrect. In common usage the word means the thoughts and feelings, memories, perceptions, dreams, imaginations, etc. playing in the mind. We have learned that consciousness is a "stream," a thought flow. But Consciousness is that in which mental and emotional phenomena rise and fall, the container of the thoughts. It is immovable. The discrimination that one practices might proceed with the continuous subtraction of the thoughts from their container, consciousness, or me. That I am conscious is the important fact, not what I am conscious of. Ignorance is simply the confusion of myself with the phenomena arising and falling within the scope of my limitless awareness, "That which sees but which the mind cannot see."[115]

Two words that cement this idea of Consciousness are **sentient** and **insentient**. Consciousness is alive, aware. The three bodies are insentient, unconscious.

That and **this**: these words are helpful in sorting out the riddle of identity. The experiences arising in meditation are "that," meaning away from oneself. The Self, I, is "this." "This" indicates nearness. "The nearest of the near," says scripture. What's nearer to you than you?

The meaning of the words one uses to liberate oneself needs to be clear. The most famous *Upanishadic* proclamation, "You are That," seems to contradict the knowledge that "that" is not me. In this case the Self, "you," seems to be a "that" because it is referred to from the plane of the ego where it appears as an object. When we meditate, we meditate on objects. There is no meditation without objects. If the reflection of the Self appears in the *sattvic* mind we need to know that what we're seeing is really us, not an independent light. Prolonged meditation on the Light will of course ultimately reveal the identity between the meditator and the object of meditation.

Inquiry requires a flexible, scientific, non-dogmatic state of mind. For example, the Self is defined as "the nearest of the near" and "the farthest of the far." It is described as "within" and "without," infinitely huge and infinitely small. When I can properly identify the non-existent ego[116] and the very existent Self, I can understand how two apparently contradictory facts are not contradictions at all. From the ego's point of view, the Self is non-existent, and therefore "the farthest of the far," space being a metaphor for ignorance. From the Self's point of view, the Self is "the nearest of the near." In knowledge there is no distance.

---

114. We've already determined that Self-knowledge is not "intellectual." But enlightenment is useless if it doesn't establish the thought "I am limitless awareness" in the intellect, because the Self functions through the intellect. If I experience limitlessness at a deeper or transcendental level but have no intellectual comprehension of it, the experience will only serve to provoke a conflict within myself.

115. Verse 127 of *Vivekachoodamani* by Shankaracharya.

The concepts of **action** and **inaction**, doing and being, are extremely useful in identifying the Self and the ego. As I sit in Silence, I experience a great deal of activity. If the senses are working, I notice all the sounds and movements in physical reality. If inactive, I notice the unceasing movement of the mind. These movements take place in the context of non-movement, i.e. Consciousness. The Self is the consciousness of the movements, that which us allows us to evaluate the movements. Action, like thought and feeling, is unconscious. It has no idea it is known by you, the meditator, the Self.

The scriptural statement that "the one who knows action in inaction and inaction in action is indeed wise"[117] means that there is no real distinction between what is moving and what is not, that the appearance of movement is caused by using the instrument of knowledge, the mind. In fact the "knowledge" that things are moving is ignorance, produced, like the mirage, by identification with the mind. When one identifies completely with the Self, all movement stops, a phenomenon often referred to as "the still point." The "inaction" in action is the realization that actionless awareness is the content of every activity. Nothing happens on its own, although the Self does not seem to be involved in our actions. Yet activity implies Consciousness. The sun, for example, cannot be said to be directly involved in any of my personal actions, insofar as I can do things in the dead of night or a completely sunless place, like a cave under the earth. However, if the sun stops shining, all activity on the earth eventually stops. The action one sees in inaction is the knowledge that the potential for action exists in the Self, that its mere presence generates the immense energy that creates, maintains and destroys the whole universe.

Cause and **effect**: What is the source of all the phenomena witnessed in meditation? As I sit in the Silence, I might profitably attempt to trace the thoughts, the effects, to their source. When I do so, I see that they are emerging out of and dissolving back into the Silence. And what is the source of the Silence? Me, awareness, the knowing principle, that because of which the objects and the Silence are known.

When the texts tell us that the Self is all-pervasive like space, it means that everything that happens in the mind is pervaded by Consciousness. Before any

116. The water in the mirage metaphor shows how it is possible to identify the non-existence of something. Perhaps we might profitably modify the teaching of the non-existence of ego to say that it both is and is not. Although it exists as an experience, it does not exist as reality.

117. The *Bhagavad Gita*.

mental phenomenon appears, Consciousness is there. Consciousness illumines it as it plays in the mind and supercedes its disappearance. When I carefully examine each and every experience/thought by holding my attention on it, it resolves back into me, the awareness.

Limited and **limitless, measurable** and **immeasurable,** and **beginningless** and **endless**: experience is limited; it begins and ends. Thought is limited. Feeling is limited. Perception is a meaningless, temporally discrete activity. It can be evaluated because the Self knows its beginning and end, and transcends its relationship to other perceptions. The Self, however, is an unlimited experiencer. When you meditate, try to find your limits. You cannot. Therefore you are immeasureable.

Describable and **indescribable**: you can describe objects, but you cannot describe the Self, because it has no form.

Incomplete and **complete**: the objects are incomplete; they begin and end and are made up of parts. The ego, for example, is just a fiction created in memory by stringing together many discrete experiences and assuming they belong to some individual. The expectant part of the psyche is the ego and its expectations are proof of its incompleteness. The Self is free of preferences and expectations because it is complete.

Pure and **impure**: what is made up of parts is impure, what is partless is pure. The Self is a partless whole. The mind is impure, a continually changing assortment of experiences.

Sound and **soundless**: the physical world and the mind are continually vibrating. These vibrations occur in soundlessness, the Silence.

Agitation and **peace**: the body and mind are continually disturbed because they are at the mercy of their causes and the effects. The Self is peaceful because it is one homogenous mass of awareness, pervading everything. Nothing affects it, just as space is unaffected by the objects and activities taking place within it.

Pleasure and **pain**: the mind is painful because it is in constant conflict with itself and the world around. The Self is pure pleasure because it is not in conflict with anything. This is why it is also called bliss or joy. Enlightenment is not the emotional feeling of joy, even though the emotions may be elevated when the Self is known. It is peace, wholeness.

Irreducible: discrimination means that as I study the subjective world opened up by my inquiry, I bring my attention to various experienceable phenomena which I compare to the Self. And the more I inquire into a phenomenon, like my ego, the more I discover that it is dismissable. It cannot stand scrutiny, a fact that leads me to conclude that it is not real. When I perform an analysis on my Self I cannot remove it.

Self-luminous, self-supporting: all objects, the senses and mind included, operate with borrowed light. The Self shines on them and they are knowable. As I explore my Self, I discover that it is self-luminous, continually generating and maintaining its light from within itself. Knowledge that I am that light means that I am a light unto myself. I do not need existential validation from anyone or anything.

Ever-free: this self-validating, self-luminous nature of the Self is known as *moksa*, freedom. I do not depend on anything other than myself for my existence. When I think of myself as a body or mind, I condemn myself to a circumscribed existence.

A cursory study of a few Vedantic texts will provide the meditator with a long list of terms that help to discriminate the Self from the not-Self. Lest the meditator reject the idea of using relative knowledge as a means of Self-realization because it is merely "intellectual," he or she needs to be reminded that the relative means of knowledge, the Self and the not-Self, is only a tool the purified intellect uses to realize the Self. When it dissolves the belief in oneself as a limited being, it drops out of consciousness. From this point on, the belief "I am limitless awareness" has "become" a fact.

Moreover, if I'm using ideas to guide my inquiry, I need to make sure that I understand how to use them. For this I need discipline and a teacher, since inquiry is the application of knowledge. I need discipline because ignorance is tenacious. I need a teacher because I need to learn how to think. **The technique of inquiry is not merely asking questions, but using the logic inherent in the impersonal, scriptural way of reasoning to destroy ignorance.** The logic is presented throughout this text. A rare someone with a purified, sophisticated mind and the determination to use the method of inquiry might successfully remove his or her ignorance solely on the basis of a deep study of this and other texts, but the best way by far is to subject oneself to the teachings at the feet of a realized soul. Surrendering oneself to this means is the most efficient and the traditional way to realize the Self. During this style of *sadhana* the student's and the teacher's minds become attuned and the teachings constituting the inquiry become the natural way of thinking.[118]

I Am the Means of Knowledge

But study at the feet of a master does not always do the trick. The spiritual world is little more than tens of thousands of dedicated inquirers who have subjected themselves to copious teachings at the feet of enlightened masters – yet find themselves unenlightened. Furthermore, even when it seems the teacher is removing the student's ignorance, the student applying the teachings to his or her own mind at the time of teaching actually removes the ignorance. The teacher and teachings are two factors in a more complex situation. If the teacher could do it alone, the whole world would be enlightened by now. Likely as not enlightenment happens outside the formal teaching situation in a still and private moment as a result of a patient and careful application of the method of inquiry – when the meditator discovers "I am the means of knowledge."

Knowledge does not happen on its own. It needs an instrument. For example, sounds coming in through the ears reach the organ of hearing in the mind, causing it to vibrate. But the vibrations mean nothing until they are interpreted. Interpretation of experience depends on what one knows. And knowledge cannot happen without Consciousness. Therefore Consciousness is the ultimate means of knowledge.

The perception of events and objects in dreams raises an epistemological problem: How are they known? If the physical senses are inactive, how are sounds or images perceived in the dream? True, dream senses and dream mind experience dream objects, but how are the dream senses and mind known? They are illumined by the dream "light." Because the physical eyes are closed, no light is going to leak into the dream. The only other possible source is Consciousness, the dream "light," operating as the means of knowledge.

In the waking state, many subtle thoughts and not-so-subtle emotions are experienced. How are they known? By Consciousness. Who or what is that Consciousness? It is me, the meditator, the one without whom no meditation can take place. When I experience ego transcendence, how do I know ego transcendence? When I experience Divine love, how do I know what I am experi-

118. While the *satsang*, or "conscious company," style of *sadhana* is becoming increasingly popular and may deliver an "experience" of the Self, it does not produce enlightened beings wholesale, if at all, because very few are actually qualified to inquire and because the teachings are typically carried out in an unnatural and contrived manner, often as expensive weekend courses run by admittedly unenlightened cultish trainers who are dependent in some way on the seminars for their livelihood and who seem more inclined to whip up desire for experience than to encourage rational and open-minded inquiry. It should be noted that nearly every human activity can produce an experience of the Self and that experience is only as useful as the ego's ability to understand its value. The failure to understand the value of the Self accounts for the fact that Self experience is fleeting, like every supposedly not-Self experience.

encing? When I talk about my joys and sorrows, how do I know that I have a "me," an ego? I know because I am the means of knowledge.

The ego is not a valid means of knowledge, although it tries to pass for one. **The "knowledge" we get through ego is simply skewed interpretation of experience showing up as beliefs and opinions.** The experiences of waking egolessness and deep sleep give lie to the idea that "I," as ego, am a means of knowledge to be counted on because knowledge is happening – but the ego is not its means. In deep sleep two bits of knowledge operate: "I am limitless bliss" and "I am ignorant." In waking egolessness the knowledge "I am egoless" operates. To know that I am egoless, I need a means other than the ego. And that means is me, Consciousness.

Even the teacher and the scripture are not self-validating means, because they depend on ignorance. And ignorance depends on me, awareness. How far is ignorance from me? No matter what I know or do not know, I know or do not know it only in awareness. For example, if I claim I am unenlightened, what is my means of knowledge? If my means is simply an opinion or a belief about my existential status, my claim cannot withstand inquiry. In fact my ignorance is illumined by the same means that sheds light on my enlightenment – my Self. Knowledge and ignorance, enlightenment and endarkenment are merely objects of knowledge that do not exist apart from me, the Self.

The popular discussion of who is and who isn't enlightened means nothing without an inquiry into the means of knowledge. Since the Self, the means of knowledge, is never unenlightened, the question is moot from its point of view. How something that is enlightened by nature can apparently become unenlightened and then feel the need to re-enlighten itself is one of the spiritual world's most perplexing questions, one that only resolves itself when the means of knowledge sheds light on the dream that one is unenlightened.

Moreover, if we define enlightenment as an ego shedding its ignorance of its Self-nature, at the time of enlightenment it will have "become" the means of knowledge. As mentioned before, "becoming" means that the ego was the Self all along, not that the ego is transformed into the Self through a special experience, unless that "experience" is insight or knowledge. Those who perpetuate the belief that ego transformation is enlightenment do spiritual culture a disservice. Additionally, the reverence and respect accorded enlightened beings is also undeserved, because enlightenment is nothing other than a return to the sane and natural state. Touting one's enlightenment only calls attention to a lengthy and embarrassing stay in ignorance.

The experience of shedding ignorance might be more profitably described as waking up. When I wake up I don't become somebody else, I simply trade the idea of myself as a dreamer for the idea of myself as a waker. In fact the waker and the dreamer are the same person, but seem to be separate entities because of their association with the state of consciousness in which they find themselves at the moment.

Who Am I?

A modern formulation of the method of Self-inquiry, an ancient Vedic technique called *vichara*, was brought to the attention of the Western world by Ramana Maharshi, a popular sage who lived in the first half of the twentieth century and who is often erroneously thought to be its author.

Since Self-experience is not in short supply insofar as the experiencer, the experienced objects and the experiencing is the Self, the question of happiness, enlightenment, can be solved, again not by seeking a particular experience of the Self, but by looking into the ego, the experiencer. The ego, like everything else in the creation, is a peculiar phenomenon. On one hand, it seems to be a very real entity, me, but when we inquire into it, we can never conclusively locate it.

Knowledge, Not Ego, Makes the Inquiry

If the inquiry is going to be successful the ego cannot be the one to make it. One style of inquiry tries to directly isolate or objectify the ego, to see it as not-Self. If this is not possible, then the meditator might inquire thus: my hand is an object; I see it; but where do I experience it? Do I experience it "out there" away from me or do I experience it in me? If I experience it "out there" in objective reality, my experience of it would interfere with the object or others' experience of the object. But this is not the case. Hundreds of people can experience a film, but the film is unaffected. Therefore there is no distance between me and the objects of my experience, just as there is no distance between the dream and the dream-me. How far is the knowledge of the object from the experience of the object? The knowledge arises simultaneously with the experience. Where is the knowledge experienced? In my mind or in me? Is my mind, my knowledge, apart from me or is it in me? What is the relationship between me and my experiences, between me and my knowledge? They seem to be me, but they also seem to be not-me. Have I "become" my experiences, my knowledge? When I illumine another object, like a tree, I see the tree as it is and don't confuse it with my hand. Why? Because there is no trace of my hand left in me, awareness, when I switch from the hand-thought to the tree-thought. Though the thoughts are me, I am free of the thoughts. Though experience is me, I am free of experience.

This inquiry applies to any object, including the ego and the Silence. How far is the ego from me? It is me. How far is the Silence from me. It is me.

The idea of inquiry into the "I-thought" dovetails nicely with another ancient and effective meditation technique, *vipassana*, or insight meditation. A *vipassana* meditator is trained to make a rigorous observation of all the events taking place in the gross and subtle bodies to prove that they happen automatically and impersonally. When their appearance and disappearance is not carefully observed, they are unconsciously thought to belong to an "I" – but careful observation shows that no such "I" exists. Additionally, the meditator discovers that the mental reaction to the object occurs simultaneously with the object and that no person is involved in it.

So who is this non-existent person and how does it come about? This non-existent person comes into being because we ceaselessly identify our selves with the body and mind. And the way to break the identification with the body-mind is to first discriminate the objects from the subject, the "I," and then discriminate the "I" from the Self. Ramana says, "There is an absolute Self from which a spark proceeds as from a fire. The spark is called the ego. In the case of an ignorant man, it identifies itself with an object simultaneously with its (the object's) rise. It cannot remain independent of such association with objects. **The association is *ajnana*, or ignorance, and its destruction is the object of our efforts (inquiry).**"[119]

Separating the ego "I" from the objects may result in apparently contradictory experiences. One may discover that either the "I" cannot stand without objects (that it dissolves when separated from them) or that the "I" precedes the objects and remains when separated from them. In the first instance, the meditator need not inquire further, because the ego will be seen for what it is (or isn't) and the Self realized by default. In the second case, the meditator needs to continue the inquiry until the ego dissolves under intense scrutiny. Seeing that there is no "I" obviously changes my idea of myself. At the moment of seeing, I am forced to take myself as the Seer, the one who knows that there is no "I." If there is an "I" very little reasoning is required to realize that I am its source, since it doesn't exist unless I illumine it.

---

119. Ramana, one of the authorities on Self-realization, is pointing out that the primary purpose of inquiry is the destruction of ignorance, not the gaining of Self experience.

Once I have a fix on the Self, I need to keep my attention on it without wavering.[120] Ramana again: "To hold to It with effort is *vichara* (inquiry)." The purpose of keeping attention steady on the Self is to dissolve ignorance, the association of the Self with the "I-thought" or other objects. If we apply the "who am I?" idea, we come up with an interesting question: Who is holding attention on what? Is someone other than the Self meditating on the Self? Or if we formulate our inquiry in terms of the means of knowledge, we need to ask how the Self is known. Knowledge of it by something other than it can't be enlightenment, since we have non-dual factors, a subject and an object. When knowledge or realization takes place we see that it is the Self apparently meditating on the Self. **In reality no meditation exists, because the Self is non-dual.** "The Self meditating on the Self" is simply the language of experience masquerading as knowledge.

When the discrimination between the Self and the not-Self destroys the ego's belief in separateness, Self-realization takes place and the practice of meditation "becomes" the "state of meditation," effortless awareness. As time passes, the discrimination slowly moves from the forefront to the background of the mind, where it operates constantly and effortlessly to keep the mind peaceful and happy, a situation similar to the knowledge of one's name, which is not continually operating in the conscious mind but which appears in consciousness at a moment's notice should the need arise.

The transition from the experience of the Self to the knowledge that "I am the Self" is assured when Self-realization takes place – although it may take time for the vestiges of dualistic thinking to fade away. As the purified, inquiring subtle body looks inward at the Self and continually discriminates between the Self and the not-Self, the distinction between it and the Self starts to fade, a realization often described as ego death. And one day, without fanfare, **a very subtle shift in vision occurs and the meditator realizes that he or she is no longer meditating on the Self but has "become" the Self observing the apparent meditator.**

Three verses from Shankara's *Atma Bodh*[121] describe this point in the meditative journey from slightly differing perspectives in the language of experience. "The meditator should 'merge' the entire world of objects in the Self alone, experi-

---

120. In the context of this discussion, I am defining the holding to the Self or Silence as meditation, and *vichara* (inquiry) as the discrimination between the Self and the not-Self.

121. An eighth-century Vedantic text whose title in English is *Self-Knowledge*.

encing it as uncontaminated as the sky." The "merger" referred to is accomplished by withdrawing attention from the mind, based on a discrimination between the Self and the not-Self. The idea of action, "merging," enters the picture because there are apparently two separate objects, the Self and the not-Self. The state of deep sleep, which is a fitting if somewhat provocative symbol of enlightenment, is only accessible when the ego and its objects have "merged" or dissolved into sleep. As long as the waking ego is obsessing and ruminating on the day's experiences or worrying about tomorrow, sleep will not come. Similarly, in the peak moments of meditation, the Self remains unknown as long as attention is fixed on the silent mind. When attention is withdrawn from the mind, the Self is known purely, "uncontaminated like the sky," and the meditator, who was formerly the subject, "becomes" just another object in me, awareness. "Becomes," another action word, simply means that the subject and object were already one.

The Seeker Is the Sought

The second verse says, "No distinctions, like knower, knowledge and object of knowledge, exist in the Self. It is endless bliss shining alone." An alternative translation can be "it is endless shining" because bliss is not different from endlessness. The idea of shining refers to the Self's nature as Consciousness, and aloneness means that the Self depends on nothing but itself. When this realization becomes a hard and fast understanding, there is absolutely nothing more left to do on any level, spiritual or otherwise. Even the feeling that the world needs to be enlightened dissolves as doing "changes" to being.

The third verse puts it like this: "When the ego dissolves, the Enlightened are absorbed into the all-pervading Reality, like water into water and light into light." Self-absorption is not a physical or psychological process, but is again the language of experience attempting to express the dissolution of the cloud of unknowing covering the ego. Why are the ego and the Self one? The Self is formless awareness, and the ego is awareness in a form. Awareness in a form is awareness, in the way that water in waves is identical to water in the ocean.

Is That It?

So far so good. I am enlightened. What is next? There is no "next," because the spiritual path branches off in infinite directions from this point.

Perhaps the most common Sanskrit word describing enlightenment is *moksa*, liberation. As the Self, one is always above the mind and no longer subject to its dictates. Therefore the decision about what comes next is completely unsupervised, an often scary idea insofar as enlightenment is thought to sanction anything – including immoral behavior. However, except for the rare case of the one who realizes the Self before most negative *vasanas* have been purified, enlightenment mitigates against exploitation of others – because there are no "others." No one in his or her right mind will misuse or harm himself or herself.

Conventional wisdom in all its ignorance has it that enlightenment equals sainthood, the logic being that the perfect Self should behave perfectly. Fair enough, but who is to define "perfect" behavior? Enlightenment cannot be equated with sainthood, because the question of enlightened action depends on the nature of the vehicle through which the Self functions. Without a vehicle, the Self cannot act. For example, electricity flowing through a light bulb produces light. Functioning through a stereo it produces sound, through a heater heat. If all the *samskaras* are exhausted, physical death ensues since *samskaras* are needed to keep the body functioning. And indeed, in cases where enlightenment has come after a rigorous purification of the *samskaras* and the meditator refuses to build new ones, the body falls off. If only *sattvic samskaras* are left, consistently saintly behavior will manifest, but if traces of *rajas* and *tamas* remain, one's actions will be tainted with selfishness.

In the long run, selfishness will eventually disappear because the logic of enlightenment – that we are all one – mitigates against it. In the meantime, however, others are often confused because the behavior seems to contradict the knowledge of oneness. To the enlightened, however, residual *vasanas* are non-binding and can safely be allowed to play out.

Enlightenment Sickness

Traces of *rajas* and *tamas* in the ego are carcinogenic cells in the subtle body that can metastasize into a nasty cancer called enlightenment sickness. To avoid this disease the enlightened should continue to vigorously purify until only *sattvic samskaras* remain.

Stated plainly, enlightenment sickness occurs when the ego is allowed to co-opt the enlightenment based on an unexamined memory of past insufficiencies. An ego afflicted with this malady knows it is the Self **and wants the world to know it.** Most who realize the Self in a short time without participating wholeheartedly in an established and respectable lineage fall ill immediately. Enlightenment sickness is easy to diagnose. Its most obvious symptom is the burning need to convince others that they are in the presence of greatness. This ego can become so grandiose that it will readily put down the great masters of the past, Christ and Buddha, for example, to create the impression that the world is now blessed with the ultimate spiritual savior. Or that the elements and world events are under its conscious control. The speed with which the newly enlightened rush out to save the world is an equally obvious symptom. Enlightening the world (for its own good) invariably involves collecting devotees, setting up tax-exempt institutions that are meant to help others to enlightenment and keep the cash at home, rushing around the world conducting expensive retreats, seminars and intensives, and advertising in New Age publications or starting up magazines and newsletters featuring glowing testimonials about the tremendous power of the *guru*, with photos of the same surrounded by wholesome middle-class people smiling from ear to ear. All this is meant to serve as evidence of the *guru's* oceanic compassion, but likely as not the whole show is orchestrated by a greedy, power-hungry ego that is incapable of refraining from capitalizing on its happiness.

Another verse[122] from *Atma Bodh* addresses this issue: "When the discriminator transcends the relative plane and realizes the Self, he or she 'becomes' the Self, and should cease to identify with all objects."

Enlightened or not, contacting the objects in other than a dispassionate and discriminating spirit will compromise the *sattvic* quality of the mind. The author's admonition, concealed beneath the matter-of-fact words "discard identification with all objects" (read: experience), cautions the enlightened to avoid arrogance in evaluating the power of residual *samskaras* – because the tendency at this stage favors throwing caution to the winds and making up for lost time by achieving in happiness what one had formerly failed to achieve in unhappiness. But the belief that one can have one's cake and eat it too is evidence of an unpurified ego. Little by little, in the most innocent and imperceptible way, one can become re-identified with ego and its *karma*, and wake up endarkened one day. So to avoid a fall, "discard identification with all objects."[123]

Self-realization and a vigorous *sadhana* effortlessly purify personality dross, leaving a shining, spacious mind capable of accommodating the spiritual impulses now flooding in from the Self. Acting on these loving impulses creates *vasanas* that become the foundation of a "new" personality. Formerly rigid and

---

122. This is a controversial verse because it contradicts the conventional wisdom that the ego has to completely die for enlightenment to occur. Depending on the state of the *samskaras*, which differs from individual to individual, the ego "death" that permits Self-realization lasts for varying periods. If the re-emergent ego fails to get knowledge, it returns to *samsaric* experience and bondage. If it understands itself to be the Self, and the knowledge is "firm," that is, unforgettable, it may still have to deal with a few well-entrenched *vasanas*. The verse reminds the meditator not to get identified with them.

habitual, it becomes soft, sweet, flexible and relaxed. The intellect, burnished in the fire of discrimination, becomes brilliant. The heart, merged with the universal Heart, pours out pure love, and the body becomes an energetic channel for expressing the Self in action.

123. The knowledge "I am the Self" sticking in the mind, not the mind's contact with objects, is the crux of enlightenment. Meditators who realize the Self and behave indiscriminately compromise their enlightenment because the mind can recloud — obscuring the knowledge. Only after a period that depends on the power of the individual's *samskaras* — when the knowledge is absolutely unshakable — can the individual contact objects with impunity. At this point, the need to contact objects or engage in activities has been effaced, so the question is moot. After this, even if stray *vasanas* are put into play, they don't affect the knowledge.

Made in the
USA
Monee, IL